Stavisht
(Stavyshche, Ukraine)

Translation of
Stavisht

Original Book Edited by: Aharon Weissman

Originally published in New York 1961

JewishGen

מרכז עולמי לגנאלוגיה יהודית

The Global Home for Jewish Genealogy

A Publication of JewishGen, Inc.
Edmond J. Safra Plaza, 36 Battery Place, New York, NY 10280
646.494.5972 | info@JewishGen.org | www.jewishgen.org

MUSEUM OF
JEWISH HERITAGE
A LIVING MEMORIAL
TO THE HOLOCAUST

Stavisht (Stavyshche, Ukraine)
Translation of *Stavisht*

Copyright © 2023 by JewishGen, Inc. All rights reserved.
First Printing: March 2023, Adar 5783
Second Printing: May 2023, Sivan 5783

Editor of Original Yizkor Book: Aharon Weissman
Project Coordinator: Vivian M. Linderman
Cover Design: Irv Osterer
Layout: Jonathan Wind
Name Indexing: Stefanie Holzman
Translated by: Ida Cohen Selavan

Printed in the United States of America by Lightning Source, Inc.

Library of Congress Control Number (LCCN): 9781954176676

ISBN: 978-1-954176-67-6 (hard cover: 122 pages, alk. paper)

About JewishGen.org

JewishGen, an affiliate of the Museum of Jewish Heritage - A Living Memorial to the Holocaust, serves as the global home for Jewish genealogy.

Featuring unparalleled access to 30+ million records, it offers unique search tools, along with opportunities for researchers to connect with others who share similar interests. Award winning resources such as the Family Finder, Discussion Groups, and ViewMate, are relied upon by thousands each day.

In addition, JewishGen's extensive informational, educational and historical offerings, such as the Jewish Communities Database, Yizkor Book translations, InfoFiles, Family Tree of the Jewish People, and KehilaLinks, provide critical insights, first-hand accounts, and context about Jewish communal and familial life throughout the world.

Offered as a free resource, JewishGen.org has facilitated thousands of family connections and success stories, and is currently engaged in an intensive expansion effort that will bring many more records, tools, and resources to its collections.

Please visit https://www.jewishgen.org/ to learn more.

Executive Director: Avraham Groll

About the JewishGen Yizkor Book Project

Yizkor Books (Memorial Books) were traditionally written to memorialize the names of departed family and martyrs during holiday services in the synagogue (a practice that still exists in many synagogues today).

Over the centuries, as a result of countless persecutions and horrific atrocities committed against the Jews, Yizkor Books (Sefer Zikaron in Hebrew) were expanded to include more historical information, such as biographical sketches of famous personalities and descriptions of daily town life.

Following the Holocaust, the idea of remembrance and learning took on an urgent and crucial importance. Survivors of the Holocaust sought out other surviving residents of their former towns to memorialize and document the names and way of life of those who were ruthlessly murdered by the Nazis. These remembrances were documented in Yizkor Books, hundreds of which were published in the first decades after the Holocaust.

Most of these books were published privately, or through landsmanshaftn (social organizations comprised of members originating from the same European town or region) that still existed, and were often distributed free of charge. Sadly, the languages used to document these crucial histories and links to our past, Yiddish and Hebrew, are no longer commonly understood by a significant percentage of Jews today. As a result, JewishGen has undertaken the sacred responsibility of translating these books into English so that the culture and way of life of these communities will be preserved and transmitted to future generations.

In 1986, a group of farsighted JewishGenners started a project to pool their efforts together in groups based upon their ancestors from each town and donate money to get the Yizkor books of their ancestral towns translated into English. As the translated material became available, it was made accessible for free at www.JewishGen.org/Yizkor. Hardcover copies can be purchased by visiting https://www.jewishgen.org/Yizkor/ybip.html (see below).

It is our hope that the translation of these books into English (and other languages) will assist the countless Jewish family researchers who are so desperately seeking to forge a connection with their heritage.

Director of JewishGen Yizkor Book Project: Lance Ackerfeld

About JewishGen Press

JewishGen Press (formerly the Yizkor Books-in-Print Project) is the publishing division of JewishGen.org, and provides a venue for the publication of non-fiction books pertaining to Jewish genealogy, history, culture, and heritage.

In addition to the Yizkor Book category, publications in the Other Non-Fiction category include Shoah memoirs and research, genealogical research, collections of genealogical and historical materials, biographies, diaries and letters, studies of Jewish experience and cultural life in the past, academic theses, and other books of interest to the Jewish community.

Please visit https://www.jewishgen.org/Yizkor/ybip.html to learn more.

Director of JewishGen Press: Joel Alpert
Managing Editor - Jessica Feinstein
Publications Manager - Susan Rosin

Notes to the Reader

The images in the original book were reproduced from photographs from the time of the first edition. These reproductions were already of poor quality, being pre-war and at least 30 or more years old. As a result, the images in the book are the best achievable.

The original book can be seen online at the Yiddish Book Center and New York Public Library websites.

> Yiddish Book Center: www.yiddishbookcenter.org - Search their Yizkor Book collection using the term, Stavishtsh or Stavische

> New York Public Library Digital Collections: digitalcollections.nypl.org – Search using the Polish spelling of Stavyshche, Stawiszcze

Stavisht victims of the Shoah can be found online using the Digital Collections of Yad Vashem – World Holocaust Remembrance Center website at www.yadvashem.org. Search the Shoah Names Database by either family name or location.

JewishGen Resources – www.jewishgen.org

This book, and other JewishGen Press publications, is available for purchase on the JewishGen website. The list of available publications including ordering information may be found on the JewishGen Press Publications webpage. To easily find this page, do an Internet search on: JewishGen Press Publications.

For additional information on the town of Stavisht, use the Town Finder search on JewishGen which will lead you to other resources including the Stavisht Kehilalink website.

Cover Photos Credits and Captions

Front Cover: Photos

> First Row (left to right):
> *Aharon Weissman, Efrayim Mazur, Hanah Shohet, Meir Shohet.*

> Second Row (left to right):
> *Leah Mazur, Moshe Leyb Kanski, the mother of Leah Mazur, Rabbi Yitshak Avraham Haysinski.*

> Third Row (left to right):
> *Reb Levi son of Eliezer Menahem Spekter, Eliahu Shohet, Pesi Shohet, Feyge Shohet.*

Front Cover: Background and artwork

> Irv Osterer

Front Cover Yiddish reads, in English:

> What I Remember About Stavishtshe.

Back Cover:

> What I Remember About Stavisht - Excerpt (edited) from Meir Spektor's article.

Geopolitical Information

Stavyshche, Ukraine is located at 49°23' N 30°12' E and 74 miles S of Kyiv

	Town	District	Province	Country
Before WWI (c. 1900):	Stavyshche	Tarashcha	Kiev	Russian Empire
Between the wars (c. 1930):	Stavyshche	Kiev	Ukraine SSR	Soviet Union
After WWII (c. 1950):	Stavyshche	Tarashcha	Kiev	Soviet Union
Today (c. 2000):	Stavyshche	Stavyshche	Kiev	Ukraine

Alternate Names for the Town:

Stavishche [Ukr, Rus], Stavisht [Yid], Stawiszcze [Pol], Stawyszcze, Stavische, Stavishcha, Stavysce

Nearby Jewish Communities:

Zhashkiv 10 miles SSW
Pyatyhory 12 miles W
Volodarka 16 miles NW
Tarashcha 18 miles NE
Vynohrad 19 miles ESE
Nastashka 19 miles NNE
Kivshovata 20 miles ENE
Boyarka 21 miles E
Konela 22 miles S
Buky 23 miles SSE

Tetiyev 24 miles W
Rokytne 25 miles NNE
Lukashivka 25 miles SW
Sokolivka 26 miles S
Medvin 26 miles E
Tsibulev 27 miles SW
Bila Tserkva 28 miles N
Ivan'ky 30 miles SSE
Lysyanka 30 miles ESE
Ryzhanivka 30 miles SE

Jewish Population in 1900: 3,917

Map of Ukraine showing the location of **Stavyshche**

Table of Contents

Stavisht

Stavyshche, Ukraine

49°23' / 30°12'

Translation of *Stavisht*

Edited by Aharon Weissman

**Published in New York, 1961 by
The Stavisht Society**

Acknowledgments

**Project Coordinator
Vivian M. Linderman**

**Translated from Yiddish
by Ida Cohen Selavan**

*Our sincere appreciation to Robert A. Barnes
for permission to use this material.*

Note: The original Yiddish book can be viewed through the Digital Collections at the New York Public Library. Search using the Polish spelling of Stavyshche, Stawiszcze. The Ukrainian edition is available on Google Books.

Introduction by Ida Selavan-Schwarcz Reminiscences, Purim, March 2, 1999

Today is Purim in our town (in Jerusalem, a walled city, it will be celebrated tomorrow). Today is my late mother's 109th birthday. She was born in Stavisht on Purim in 1890 and was named Esther Malka (Queen Esther) for that reason. She lived through the events described in the second article and would sometimes talk about them. However, my father told us more, and I am so sorry my brother and I did not listen more carefully. So many of his stories are simply garbled memories. I am sure that there are many people like me who wish they had asked more questions and listened more closely.

I chose this particular article because it gives an overview of life before the pogroms and is very well written. I was told that the author later worked for the New York Times. I tried to track him down, but the personnel department of the Times was not forthcoming. Many of the names he mentions as among the intelligentzia of Stavisht are familiar to me.

Yosef Wilfand, for example, was one of the founders of Kibbutz Ein Hashofet and his widow, Bella, still lives there. Avraham Zeiger was one of the founders of Hashomer Hatzair in the United States. He is buried in Ein Hashofet. His parents, Barukh and Menya Zeiger (Singer in America), were close friends of my parents and we often visited when I was a child. My mother sometimes mentioned the Golub family. When I was a very little girl we took the subway and elevated and rode all the way to the Bronx to visit someone my mother introduced as her former teacher. It was a Mr. Golub.

Comment by Joyce Field: Ida sent me her reminiscences on Purim as she was putting the finishing touches on the two articles. I was so touched by her remembrances that I asked her if we could include them as an introduction. Ida kindly agreed. I hope the readers will concur that they add a personal touch to the words.

Introduction by Vivian M. Linderman
July, 2009

With tribute and special credit to the ever-changing world of technology, this 2009 donation of the full translation of the Stavisht Yizkor Book to JewishGen would not have been possible without email and the dedication and commitment of the following women. Their roles in preparing the translation for an online presence follow in the footsteps of the original Yizkor Book Committee to honor and memorialize the town of their ancestors and the residents who gave it life. May their memories be for a blessing and may their descendants for the generations know just a little of their life, their humor, their passions and their struggles.

VIVIAN M. LINDERMAN, granddaughter of Moshe Linderman of Zhashkov/Stavisht and Rifka Plotinsky of Stavisht; great-granddaughter of Fayvish Platinski and Ettl Margoloff (Markolowitz) of Stavisht and Josl Linderman and Toba Sklyarskij of Zhashkov/Stavisht.

KAREN I. SANDERS, granddaughter of Eisig Sanderovitch and Beile Levit; great-granddaughter of Kayla Shpitzanetzky Levit, all of Stavisht.

IDA SELAVAN SCHWARCZ, daughter of Esther Malka Spector Cohen (Kitaigorodsky); granddaughter of Nehama Tetievsky Spector and Levi Spector; great-granddaughter of Yehudit and Hirsh Tetievsky, all of Stavisht.

Translator's Notes:

The title is transcribed from the English title page. There are also Hebrew and Yiddish title pages.

"Stavisht." is transcribed thus in the text although the preferred spelling is "Stavyshche." Names of other towns will be transcribed according to usage in Where Once We Walked by Gary Mokotoff and Sallyann Sack with Alexander Sharon.

Hebrew and Yiddish words are transcribed in brackets [ ] on first occurrence. Original page numbers also are shown in brackets.

Names are transliterated as printed in the original except where information exists of correct spelling. Some names are spelled differently in different articles and some even in the same article.

Some native speakers of Yiddish use the word taykh for either river or lake. Thus, in the book it is not always clear if they are referring to the river that runs through Stavisht or the various lakes and ponds formed by the river.

סטוישצ'ה

בעריכת אהרן וייסמן

בהוצאת אגודת יוצאי סטוישצה בארצות־הברית
תל־אביב   ניו־יורק

STAVISHT

Aharon Weissman, Editor

Published by the Stavisht Society, Tel Aviv, New York

Printed in Israel, 1961
Vered Press, Tel Aviv

Translated by Ida Cohen Selavan
Cincinnati, Ohio
1994

Yizkor

May God remember the souls of our brothers, children of Israel, residents of Stavisht and vicinity, who were murdered and slaughtered and burned and asphyxiated as martyrs by the oppressors of Israel on the soil of Ukraine.

May God remember them and avenge the spilled blood of His servants.

May their souls be bound up in the bonds of eternal life.

יזכור

יזכור אלוקים נשמות אחינו בני ישראל,
תושבי סטאווישטש ובנותיה שנהרגו
ושנשחטו ושנשרפו ושנחנקו על קידוש
השם בידי צוררי ישראל על אדמת
אוקרייינה.
יזכרם אלוקים לטובה וינקום נקמת דם
עבדיו השפוך.
תהיינה נשמותיהם צרורות בצרור החיים
עד עולם.

The Committee

Arthur Schechter
(Aharon Shohet)

Honorary President

Yisrael Rubin
(Rubtshinski)

Secretary - Treasurer

Moshe Galant

Moshe Kohen

Isak Golub

Louis Lipovski

David Zaslavski

Tsadok (Charles) Mazer, of blessed memory
The founder and first president of the Stavisht Society in New York

Introduction

[Page 21/22]

Introduction to the book

by Arthur Schechter
Grand Rapids, Michigan

Arthur Schechter

I left my home town in 1907. I have been in the United States for the past 53 years.

One may ask, why did I decide, 41 years after the destruction of the Ukrainian Jewish towns, to publish a book about Stavisht? It has been so many years since the First World War and the Russian Revolution – when the Ukrainian bands robbed, murdered and destroyed Jewish life. Why have I suddenly decided to do this now?

I know that one cannot compare the events in Ukraine after the First World War with the catastrophic events of the worst misfortune in Jewish history, the destruction of European Jewry.

But it is this mass destruction of the Jewish people by the Nazis, may their names be erased, that inspired me to immortalize our martyrs from our beloved little town of Stavisht, with a book written in Yiddish, the language of our fathers and mothers.

We are the last of that generation – we have the obligation to record for future historians and for our children, the stories of our childhood lives, which, we must admit, had many shadows, but also much light and joy.

We are the living witnesses, the heirs of this holy community which lovingly planted within us the qualities of love and faith of the previous generations. We have a debt to the future, to write a memorial book about the Jewish Stavisht of the past, and to raise a monument to the martyrs ground down by the wheels of the Revolution which was supposed to bring freedom to the world. And Ukrainian hooligans exploited it to uproot Jewish settlements.

My own life in America has been similar to that of most immigrants of that time. I struggled, worked, studied a bit, got married, continued struggling, and managed to achieve my goals – a family, friends, some success in communal activity, and even a solid material base. But I have never forgotten the place where I spent the first fourteen years of my life, the small town and all those dear Jews whom we will never see again, and these memories demanded to be written down, to be recorded, so that somewhere there would remain a memorial of that time and place.

And so the years went by, year after year. I was young and I thought that I would have plenty of time, later, tomorrow, next year, what's the rush? Meanwhile the Second World War broke out, the worst catastrophe for the Jewish people, the destruction of European Jewry, pain and shame, yes, the shame is as great as the pain. How could it happen in the twentieth century, that Jews were burned up in gas ovens and the world stood by in silence? It is true that nations warred against each other, but we were killed only because we were Jews. At that time I decided to give up the idea of memorializing out town, our martyrs, and began to believe that in such a world it was better to forget. To remain silent, mute, mute like the millions of dead Jews of both world catastrophes, to mourn in silence until death would unite us with them.

I felt this way for many years, until 1949, until [after] the establishment of the beloved State of Israel. In 1949 my wife and I went to Israel, not very eagerly. I say "not very eagerly," because I pictured the State of Israel quite otherwise than what I found.

I thought it would be a small state full of Jews who were strangers to me – that is, to my generation, alien to what I had longed for, to what I had cherished in my heart for years. And here we arrived on a bright Friday into splendid sunny Jewish Tel Aviv.

As if in a dream, the magic curtain opened before my eyes, and there appeared the grand idyll of a wonderful Jewish life, beautiful houses, great institutions, with a constant tempo of building, creating. Above all the children, the sweet bright little Hayimlekh, Moshelekh, Rahelekh, Saralekh, dear, lovely, smiling children, so dear, that you want to hug and kiss them all over. It seemed to me that they were saying to me:

We are here, we are here. We are alive, we are building, to spite our enemies. We are continuing all that is dear to you. Write down the dreams of your childhood years, and of your parents and grandparents, and all the beloved Jews who live on only in your memory. We know that you and your helpers are not professional writers, but we feel that your goal is to recount the truth, to record the past generations which lived and hoped, contributed their work and yearnings and children. Yes, your small town also sent its children to help build the State of Israel... So write about your small town, the tragic end of your martyrs, and about the dreams which we have realized here, the joy of the great victory of the State of Israel, which cost us so much blood.

With this inspiration I was encouraged to take on the task in my old age of recording my memories and establishing a monument to our dear little town and to its dear community of Jews, and its few surviving heirs.

I could mention here the sorrow and pain I encountered among some landslayt [compatriots] in New York and especially in Boston, to whom our committee came for moral and financial support to realize our dream. But, writing these lines in Tel Aviv, I forgive them.

I would rather mention here the loyal comrades without whom this whole project could not have succeeded. First of all, the man for whom I have great respect and friendship, is Yisrael Rubin of New York, for his energetic work in collecting materials and funds for the book. Moshe Kohen of Philadelphia, the enthusiastic Stavisht patriot, who bombarded me with letters, and demanded responses, and against whom I often sinned by not answering all his letters. To the very sympathetic Golub brothers of New York, to Moshe Galant, David and Hava Zaslavski. To the honest, sincere, Mr. and Mrs. Lipovski, and others whom I cannot recall just now – to all of you my dear landslayt and all who participated in this book I send my blessings and wish that you merit that your children should carry on the traditions of our people and that they should keep their memories of you deep in their hearts as you do the memories of our dear Jews of Stavisht.

[Page 27/28]

The Initiators of the Book of Stavisht

by Moshe Kohen
Philadelphia, Pennsylvania

For about ten or twelve years I had been corresponding with Yisraelik Rubin (Yashke the butcher's son from Stavisht), now in New York, about how to memorialize the town of Stavisht and its Jews. We wrote back and forth on the subject, but nothing materialized.

One of our landslayt, Aharon Shohet, in America his name is Arthur Schechter, lives in [Grand] Rapids, Michigan. He is the son of Meir-Velvl Hava's. This dear man, Arthur Schechter, used to come to New York a few times a year on business, and he met with Yisraelik Rubin from time to time. Yisraelik Rubin revealed to him that he had been thinking of ways to perpetuate the memory of our Stavisht of long ago.

When Arthur Schechter heard this, he realized that he was not the only one with this idea. He was inspired to take action to bring the idea to fruition. In his correspondence with Yisraelik Rubin, he suggested that he call a meeting of landslayt and tell them about the plan.

The first meeting of landslayt to carry out the plan of publishing a memorial book for Stavisht took place on a hot Saturday night in June 1959. Fourteen people from New York participated, and a few came from outside New York, including the writer of these lines, my brother-in-law, Motl Markman of Philadelphia, and, of course, Arthur Schechter of Grand Rapids, Michigan. One cannot forget the impressive speech of our dear landsman [compatriot], Arthur Schechter, which he gave at this first meeting. How much heart and soul he put into his talk for the carrying out of this holy task. At this first meeting a committee was chosen to memorialize Stavisht and its Jews.

Arthur Schechter promised to cover 25% of the cost of publication of the memorial book. The landslayt of New York and the committee had to overcome many difficulties. Yisraelik Rubin, the secretary, deserves a special thanks for he is the life-line of the committee. We have to thank him for our success. And, of course, we must praise our dear honorary president, Arthur Schechter, for his active role in the work of publishing the book. He is a man of initiative, faith, and patience, who can achieve the most difficult goals.

Afterwards I met with Arthur Schechter and Yisraelik Rubin, the dear Stavisht activists, in Philadelphia in 1960. Although all three of us were busy with our personal affairs, the memorial book project occupied a very important and central place in our hearts and souls. For me this meeting was a spiritual experience. I felt such carefree joy, as if I were a young boy, forgetting the tens of years since we were uprooted from our home in Stavisht, and that we have been citizens of the United States for many years. Here is our dear landsman Arthur Schechter, who was but a fourteen year old boy when he came to America, and has been here for over fifty years, but he is still tied to his home town by spiritual bonds. And we landslayt, no matter where we find ourselves, are still tied heart and soul to our unforgettable old home of previous generations. Every landsman has the holy obligation of acquiring this book, which will immortalize the memory of Stavisht and its Jews and of the dear parents and grandparents who raised us with devotion and dedication.

[Page 29/30]

Stavisht Society in New York

by Yisrael Rubin

In 1907 a group of 25 Stavisht landslayt got together and founded an organization with the name "Ershter Stavishtsher Untershtitsung-Fareyn" [First Stavisht Mutual Aid Society] with Tsadok Mazer as the first president. It received a charter from New York State and continued its work until 1916. During this period some members broke away and formed a Stavisht branch of Workmen's Circle. However, with the passage of time, most of them rejoined the Society which was reorganized in 1916.

During the First World War and the Russian Revolution there were persecutions and murders of Jews in Ukraine and mass emigration to America and other countries. The residents of the small towns left their homes and businesses and all their possessions and fled. Most of the emigrants went to Romania, some to Poland, and others to Germany, England, and Palestine and other countries. When they arrived in the foreign countries, poor, without clothing, and without any livelihood, their cries for help reached the landslayt in America.

What did the Society do?

Tsadok Mazer, the president of the Society, called a conference of all the landslayt and they decided to found a relief fund. He worked day and night without rest, he and a committee of some of the members: Yosef Rabinovits, Ayzik Silverman, Louis Kien, Sam Saks, Yosef Burshteyn, Philip Ratof, Yosef Silverman, Yosef Kanski, Louie Derzshanski and others used to visit landslayt they knew every night of the week and on weekends they were able to raise a few thousand dollars.

They chose delegates and sent them to Romania and to border towns to help the emigrants with money, papers, visas and whatever they needed so that they could come to America. This was one of the noblest deeds which people could do for the suffering Jews. This continued until suddenly the doors of the countries were shut with iron curtains and they could not help them emigrate, even with money.

Our rabbi, Rabbi Yitshak Avraham Gaysinski, went from Russia to England. He was there a few years and decided to come to America, and when he arrived the Society received him warmly. At first he was in Philadelphia. A delegation of our Society went there and brought him to New York. He was made an honorary member of our Society.

I wish to add a few words about our founder and first president, Tsadok Mazer, peace upon him. He was a genial person with a good heart and soul. He loved people in general and Stavisht landslayt in particular. He was always ready to help someone in need. He often neglected his family and business in order to go help, and if he could not go himself, he would send his son, Harry Mazer who was then still a young boy.

His house was open to all, as was his heart. He used to help everyone with advice and deeds. Unfortunately he was torn from us at a young age and we miss him very much. Stavisht landslayt will never forget him, honor to his memory.

In the course of the years our Society grew in membership and now has almost 200 families. We have carried out a number of entertainments, balls, dance evenings and banquets. I remember a banquet which we had in 1948 when the State of Israel was founded. We raised money to build a house in the State of Israel in the name of the Stavisht Society of New York.

Another happening, at our banquet in 1956, we celebrated the 40th anniversary of our Society, reorganized in 1916. The banquet was held in a grand hall in the Bronx with good food and music. On this occasion we prepared a golden book with photographs in which most of the members wrote their greetings. Part of the book was devoted to memorial notices for our dear ones. We had 25 guests from various cities: Boston, Philadelphia, Connecticut, Buffalo, Chicago, Toronto, Canada and even Africa.

Our benefits include insurance policies for every member, sick benefits and other benefits for the members, and support for various organizations. We own three fully paid for cemeteries [sections], a few thousand dollars in the bank, American and Israel Bonds. We hold regular meetings every month. We have very reliable directors and our business is carried out in the most democratic fashion. We have an office in Academy Hall, on Fourteenth Street in New York, where we hold our meetings.

For the past 25-30 years, our Society has been a model for other societies. All landslayt from Stavisht should be proud to belong to our Society.

[Page 33/34]

הסוכנות היהודית לארץ־ישראל
JEWISH AGENCY EXECUTIVE JERUSALEM

וזאת התעודה
למפעל־השכון
HOUSING CERTIFICATE

לאות הוקרה על התרומה הנדיבה
IN APPRECIATION OF A
למען המגבית היהודית המאוחדת
GENEROUS CONTRIBUTION TO THE
שבביו־יורק רבתי, שנתנה על ידי
UNITED JEWISH APPEAL
OF GREATER NEW YORK

BY First Stavister Benev. Assn.

וסיעה לספוק הצורך הדחוף למתן
TO HELP MEET THE URGENT NEED FOR
דיור ומחסה לעולים החדשים בישראל
SHELTERING NEWCOMERS IN ISRAEL

One
HOUSING UNITS יחידות־דיור
HAVE BEEN DEDICATED
הוקמו לזכרון־עולם
AS A LASTING MEMORIAL

TO Stavist

1949

[Photocopy of the Housing Certificate of the State of Israel stating that the "First Stavister Benevolent Association" dedicated one housing unit "as a lasting memorial to Shavist," dated 1949.]

Memories

[Page 41-42]

Of Bygone Days

by Rabbi M. Halevi
Yavniel, Israel

If the author of the <u>Song of Songs</u> were to seek a phrase to characterize the town of Stavisht, he would certainly choose the words, I am dark but comely, daughters of Jerusalem. For indeed the outward appearance of the town was dark and dismal. If you would look at its inhabitants you would think: Here are the descendants of the exiles of ancient Judea, the signs of their wanderings and travail etched on their faces and reflected in their eyes, full of longing, deep concern for making a living, fear of the gentile, and readiness to flatter him or to be beaten.

The streets on which they lived lacked anything to please the eye. There was almost no sign of green. The rows of houses were crooked and dilapidated; there were no paved sidewalks; many of the houses had no courtyards or even gates and their floors were of clay, freshened every Sabbath eve.

The impression of poverty given by the Jewish neighborhood was underscored by its juxtaposition with the beautiful grounds surrounding the palace of the Count – the landowner. Here the houses were well built, there were well-tended gardens, lawns and flowers, peace and beauty. Here were the homes of the many officials who worked in the splendid office of the Count, involved in managing his estates.

"I am with him in misfortune." The Shekhinah [Divine Presence] too was in exile: the Bet Hamidrash [House of Study, a generic name for a synagogue; but in Stavisht, the name used for a particular synagogue], the Talnoye Kloyz [small prayer house for followers of the Hasidic rebbe of Talnoye], and the Makarov Kloyz [for followers of the Makarov rebbe] were on the second floors of shops with no boundaries between holy and secular.

"I am dark on the outside, as the tents of Kedar, but beautiful within, as the tent of Solomon." The holy congregation distinguished itself and expressed its spirituality in three ways:

A. Zionism. Every upstanding person was a Zionist. This poor community bought 200 shares of the Colonial Bank. Two thousand pounds sterling was an enormous sum in Stavisht sixty years ago. When they read in the newspaper that Dr. Herzl had said that if he had the entire sum that had been promised for the bank it would help enormously in his negotiations with the rulers of Turkey, they sent a representative to Kiev to Professor Mandelshtam to ask him for details and to tell him that if this were indeed the case, they were prepared to make inordinate sacrifices, even to sell the pillows from under their heads in order to help. The noble professor calmed them down and told them that matters had not yet come to such a pass.

The Zionists in Stavisht built their own synagogue. Their by-laws were composed and written by Yaakov Koplivitski whose Hebrew pen was that of a good scribe. I have not seen the pinkas but some of the by-laws were transmitted to me orally and they are:

- Every one who attends the synagogue regularly must buy a shekel every year.
- On the first night of Selihot [penitential prayers said from the Sunday before the New Year] the gaba'im [wardens] for the following year and the permanent seats of the worshippers would be chosen by lot.
- The gaba'im would be in charge of the budget and on Yom Kippur eve everyone was obligated to pay what he had promised according to his means. If for some reason someone refused to pay, Kol Nidre [All My Vows – opening prayer of Yom Kippur] would be delayed until the miscreant promised to annul his refusal.
- The synagogue would receive no charitable contributions.
- On Simhat Torah everyone would volunteer a donation to the Jewish National Fund according to his means.
- Next to the Reader of the Torah there would be a box in which the names of all members would be kept. The Reader would pick a name out of the box for each aliyah [a call to read from the Torah or recite a blessing]. He would put the name of one who had been called into a second box. After all of the slips of paper had been removed from the first box, he would mix them up in the second box and the aliyot [plural of aliyah] would again be assigned by lot.

What beautifully simple and egalitarian principles in the House of God!

I must here mention the names of those who left for Erets Yisrael in the days of the Second Aliyah [Jewish emigration to Palestine 1904-1914] hoping to find a way to make a living there. They were: Shelomo Solgenik, Leyb Vaisman, and later, Eliyahu the stove builder. They returned, but their attempt reflects their longing for redemption.

In his book, Mi-yamim rishonim [Early Days], A. Druyanov tells about the attempt by Yosef Kuderansky to purchase large tracts of land near Beersheva. For this purpose an organization was formed, Agudat Yisrael, and one of the branches was in Stavisht.

The Zionist spirit here was also the reason I was brought to Stavisht from Rabbi Reines yeshiva [in Lida] to serve as rabbi. To celebrate the occasion representatives from Zhashkov came to greet me and among them were Eliyahu Dayan, a member of En Ganim, and one of the founders of Nahalal, as well as his brother, Shemuel Dayan [father of Moshe], who had come from Deganya to visit his parents in Zhashkov and had stayed in the home of the Zionist rabbi for a few days.

The elders of Stavisht who were Hasidim wondered: A Litvak, a Zionist who does not belong to any Hasidic sect, how will he teach Torah? But permit me to reveal that the young man in his innocence, his ways, and his speech, quickly won the full support of the community.

B. The Talmud Torah. In those days, when the heder [one room school], in its old form, was the only popular way of education for most of the children in the Pale of Settlement, the Zionists of Stavisht established the Talmud Torah in modern form. It was in a suitable building, with a separate teacher for each class, with singing and with graduation certificates and under the supervision of the Kiev branch of the Hevrat Mefitse Haskala [Society for the Promotion of Culture among the Jews of Russia].

The first principal was Efrayim Fukson. The Talmud Torah cost its supporters a great deal of money. They were all members of the middle class who hoped that the success of the institution would bring returns on their investments. Here I should mention Yitshak Besidski invested all of his money in the venture, 800 rubles, a fortune in those days. I never heard the investors bemoan the loss of their funds.

In the book, Naftule dor, in the article on prisoners of Zion, there is mention of Riva Besidski, daughter of Yitshak, as one of those imprisoned in Siberia.

C. Prayer. I came to Stavisht from Belarus and was deeply impressed by the heartfelt liturgy of the Ukrainian Jews. Even the daily Minha [afternoon prayer] was for them a singing of Psalms.

Every synagogue in Stavisht had a paid cantor. The cantors Shemuel of the Bet Hamidrash and Efrayim of Sha'ar Tsiyon chanted beautifully. The last named was a pupil of Zaydl Rovner and knew how to read music. He organized a choir of local boys who sang on the holidays. It seems to me that this was a unique phenomenon in the area.

During the summertime, after the Sabbath, a group of "intellectuals" would gather at my home for tea and discussions. Among them was Ya'akov Tsherkas, who had a sharp mind, loved the truth, and pursued justice. We talked about current events and matters concerning Jews. I would be expected to speak on Torah and the sayings of the sages.

After the important holidays we would have meetings of "rivals," Hasidim and Zionists. There was peaceful discussion and we all sang together.

I remember one such evening, a time of enjoyment in this world. It was after Passover, spring in nature and in one's heart. We sang the sweet strains of the Tal prayer [prayer for dew] and Efrayim the cantor sang the phrase, "and you shall count from the day after Pesah," etc. One of those assembled, a rather strange man named Ya'akov, about whom it was said that he had been of little faith and had left his home and wandered in foreign places including Egypt and Erets Yisrael, returned and became a Bratslav Hasid. He danced around excitedly singing, "Praise His name in dance" and was joined by those singing and clapping their hands until he wore them out.

What a dear congregation, holy and modest! How it has been destroyed and ravished in the years of terror and murder!

[Page 45/46]

Rabbi in Stavisht for a Short Time

by Rabbi H. Isaac Reiter
Rabbi of the Home for the Aged of Brooklyn,
on Howard and Dumont Avenues

We should thank God for the loving kindness to us Russian Jews, and especially Ukrainian Jews, for allowing us to find a haven in the United States and especially in New York where there are about 2,500,000 Jews, among them many landslayt. We remember those of our landslayt who were martyred in the pogroms (about 600,000) in the years from 1919-1925, when whole towns and villages were wiped out by Petliura, Zeleny, Sokolovsky, and other bandits. Among these towns I must recall the town of Stavisht, Kiev Province. There I arrived as the son-in-law of my wife's noble and important parents, Avraham Gayfman and Sara Hirshl-Hanah's. My father-in-law was a great scholar and a prominent person in town. I served in Stavisht as a rabbi without salary, especially after the rabbi, Rabbi Yitshak Avraham who was called "Pitsie Avraham" Gaysinski had left. At that time there were about 800 families, that is about 4,500 Jews.

Stavisht was considered a fine town. It had six synagogues and a fine Talmud Torah, a Bikur Holim [visiting the sick] and a hostel for poor wayfarers. There were four ritual slaughterers of whom two, Avraham and Ya'akov, were killed by the murderers. There were honest artisans, almost all of whom were Sabbath observers, four butchers, and upstanding householders with fine families. Rabbi Gaysinski was a great scholar and was very warm and friendly and especially skilled in the legal ramifications of debt and repayment.

I left Stavisht in 1913 to become a rabbi in Pogrebishche, Kiev Province, in place of my grandfather, Rabbi Avraham Moshe Reiter, who had served there for forty years. I served there until 1929 and God helped me leave for New York, where I and my family live.

My birthplace was also destroyed as were most of the small towns of the Ukraine. It would be good if there would be cities and towns built in Israel with the names of these holy places, as a memorial for our martyred brothers and sisters. If we could write all of the events of the years between Petliura and Hitler our grief and lamentations would be indescribable.

We pray that God will bring full redemption quickly.

[Page 49/50]

Fifty Years Ago

by Professor M. Haysinski
University of Paris, France

Stavisht, Tarashcha, Zhashkov, Pyatigory, Titiyev, Shvarts-Timeh [Belaya Tserkov]...towns and hamlets, where we studied, lived, worked, often suffered, but also rejoiced with our parents, brothers, sisters, friends. I remember mostly gray and dark memories of life there, but I also remember moments of light and shining countenances as if I had lived them only yesterday.

Stavisht ...here is the "Main Street:" A wide street. On one side, before the bridge, a large pharmacy, then my friend Berl Besidski's house, a drug store, the Talnoye Kloyz, the post-office [post delivered by horses] with the first telephone in town, the Bet Hamidrash, more stores, another drugstore, the police station and then the Count's estate. This was another world with a wide boulevard, beautiful houses and gardens, where the Jewish young men and young women would promenade on a Saturday afternoon cracking sunflower seeds. This was a whole different and foreign town belonging to Count Branicki and the managers of his forests and fields, cities and towns. Nevertheless, when I visited the famous castles on the Loire in France in the 1930's (Chateaux de la Loire) and I saw that the castle in the city of Loush [Loches] belonged to Count Branicki, or his heirs, I had the urge to go in and carry on a conversation about Stavisht. After all, this was a man from back home, even though he was a Polish nobleman.

We return to our big Jewish street. On the other side was the post office, my friend Yosl's house, a big one, because his grandfather was an important egg merchant who bought and sold all over the region of Kiev to Volochisk on the Austrian border. Then came the Makarov Kloyz, the marketplace and more stores. On all sides there were other streets with small, old houses, with a lot of mud, almost all year long. In these houses lived a few wealthy people and a great many poor artisans: tailors, cobblers, small merchants, butchers, carpenters, ritual slaughterers, cantors, rope makers, teachers.

Indeed my first memories of shining countenances are of my teachers. What they taught me has little to do with what I now teach. There are other students here in Paris, but "I have learned from all my teachers." What I learned in Stavisht between the seventh and fifteenth years of my life has not been completely forgotten. And even that which I have forgotten is not completely lost, for nothing is lost in our world. Everything takes on a new form and is found sooner or later. Cast your bread upon the waters.

I especially remember Reb Leyzer and Reb Lozer. I studied Bible with the first named and Modern Hebrew with the second one. Reb Leyzer wore a long, not always clean, coat (may he forgive me in Paradise where, I am certain, he resides with all of my rebbes). He had many children and little income, quite a few students in a very small house in which his wife plucked feathers almost at the table where we read and wrote. Reb Leyzer had little patience. He was often irritated and nervous. But I am certain that no one in Stavisht knew the Bible as well as he did and no one taught it with such devotion and with such a love of the Prophets, especially of Isaiah. Honesty, justice, and peace, the ideals which the prophet had expressed with enthusiasm have rarely found an exponent as devoted as Reb Leyzer.

Reb Lozer was very different. He was certainly not much richer than his colleague, but he dressed like a maskil [enlightened Jew]; with a short clean jacket, with pince-nez, and also, it seemed to me, with a somewhat clipped beard. He was quiet and calm as he taught us Hebrew grammar, discussed Hebrew poetry, and the periodical Hatsefira, where he especially loved David Frishman's cogent and elegant articles and Nahum Sokolow's political analyses. Sometimes he would dictate difficult Hebrew texts to us. I usually wrote quite correctly. Once, however, I made an error, as did all of my classmates except for Reb Lozer's daughter, the only girl in our school. If my classmate Reb Lozer's daughter reads these lines, she should be assured that I have always had the greatest respect for her knowledge and I bow low before her.

Of all of my Stavisht teachers the greatest impression, naturally, was made by my grandfather, Rabbi Yitshak Avraham, son of Yisrael. I say "naturally" not because he was my grandfather, but because he was one of the strongest personalities I have ever known. I have met some very important people in my lifetime, but since a grandson cannot serve as a witness let me only say that my grandfather taught me Gemara [part of the Talmud] and Shulhan Arukh [Code of Laws]. Unfortunately he had little time for me and he would send me to the Sokolovka Kloyz to study by myself. What I studied there in the long afternoon hours is another story, a personal one. I have not forgotten the Sokolovka Kloyz, just as I have not forgotten the other Stavisht synagogues. There are five continents on this globe, but Stavisht had six synagogues: The Big Shul, the Bet Hamidrash, the Talnoye Kloyz, the Makarov Kloyz, the Sokolovka Kloyz, and the Zionist Kloyz. Just as every continent is different from the others, so did every one of our synagogues have its own character, its own atmosphere, its own frequenters.

We should remember that in my youth the Bet Hamidrash or the kloyz was not just a house of prayer where people came to mumble their prayers in haste, but also a center of social, cultural, and even political activity. Men would spend long hours there studying, chatting, discussing personal matters, community affairs, town politics about the slaughter house, the bathhouse, rabbis and ritual slaughterers, cantors and sextons. They would zealously discuss world politics: peace and war, Zionism and Bundism, faith and apostasy, the internal situation in Russia, the Beilis trial, the murder of Stolypin in the Kiev theater, and so on and so on.

I also knew the Talnoye Kloyz quite well. I would often go there to study, or play kvitlekh [home-made card games] with my friend Yosl, whom I have already mentioned. The Talnoye Kloyz was the most important one in Stavisht. It was the place where the "aristocracy" worshipped: men of prestige, wealth, clever merchants from important families, refined men with beautiful beards and silk kapotes [long coats].

On the other hand, the Big Shul was democratic, even proletarian. It had no rabbi or rebbe. There were many maskilim in the Zionist Kloyz, with short beards, sometimes even close-shaven, who read Hatsefira or Hazeman or the liberal Russian periodical Kievskaya Mysl'. Many of them sent their children to a modern Hebrew School where the poet Fukson taught, and some of them even sent their children to the Russian high-school.

At the beginning of this century one could meet in Stavisht people of every leaning from pious Hasidim who ate at the tables of the Skvira, Talnoye, or Sokolovka rebbes, to free thinkers and persons who would become well known in the worlds of science and politics in later years.

[Page 55/56]

My Grandfather, the Rabbi of Stavisht

by Hava Goldman
Hebron, Connecticut

Stavisht, Tarashcha Uyezd [district], Kiev Province belonged to a Polish nobleman Count Branicki. He spent most of his time abroad, but his estate manager was always in residence at the palace as were the stewards who took care of his property. They were a source of income for the local Jews.

As in all small towns, there was a marketplace in the middle of the town where the Jewish shopkeepers were. There were a few wealthy merchants who dealt in manufactured goods, from notions to groceries, but most of the Jews had small shops where they barely earned a meager living.

The best business was selling galoshes because in Stavisht only the main street from Traktave to the Count's palace was paved, but on both sides all was mud. I remember the deep mud near my grandfather's house near the Sokolovka synagogue where he prayed. One had to be an acrobat to make it from one house to another on the various boards and stones over the mud, even with galoshes.

My grandfather, Rabbi Yitshak Avraham Gasinski, was the rabbi in Stavisht for forty years and was known all over the area as "Pitsie Avraham the rabbi." Carriages would go from my birthplace Tarashcha daily to Stavisht and back. We would always go to my grandfather's house in Stavisht for the holidays. When I came I would always find a house full of people. The life of the town was centered in his home. Here came the parents of a couple to talk about a wedding, and here came a couple to get a divorce. Some people would give my grandfather their money to hold for them when they bought a house or a store. Mostly they came to the religious court. As a child I loved to look on as both sides became wearied with arguing and yelling, when my grandfather would hand them a kerchief [to symbolize acceptance of the judgment] and say to them, "If you listen to me, I shall give you my decision." My grandfather participated in every matter concerning the town. Even if someone had a headache he would go to the apothecary and ask for Pitsie Avraham's powder.

My grandfather showed his courage and devotion to his people after the Revolution, in 1918-1919, when all over the Ukraine the dreadful pogroms broke out. In the beginning, when we heard about the pogroms in the nearby towns my grandfather organized the young people of Stavisht to guard the town at night so that the local gentiles would not rob. Some of the young folk were not too eager to walk around at night, but when they saw the old rabbi doing it they were shamed into going along. But the local Jewish watch could not guard the town for long. The infamous hooligan Zeleny came with his hundreds of armed soldiers and the town was full of them.

Rabbi Yitshak-Avraham Haysinski
may the memory of the righteous be for a blessing

All the Jews locked themselves in their houses and were afraid to look out but my grandfather, heedless of my grandmother's and the children's weeping, went outside. He was immediately encircled by followers of Zeleny. He asked them to take him to the Ataman. My grandfather introduced himself to Zeleny as the rabbi of the town. Since the soldiers were guests, he wished to provide them with boots, sugar, salt, and much money on condition that they would protect the town. A miracle occurred and the Ataman liked my grandfather's suggestion.

Accompanied by two soldiers my grandfather went from house to house and collected provisions for the dear guests. The pogromchiks took the gifts and nevertheless they also robbed, but they did not kill too many people. When they left town there were a total of eight Jews murdered, and this was considered good.

Just as the Zeleny forces left they heard that a new band was coming, more dreadful than the first. Since nobody had any money or valuables left, they decided to leave town, and all the Jews, young and old, healthy and sick, started walking on foot to Volodarka, a small town not far away.

I believe that it is superfluous to describe the scene, how dreadful it was for a town full of people to leave their homes and all within, and when they came to the town of Volodarka it was no better. They discovered that Zeleny and his troops were there. Again my grandfather went to Zeleny and persuaded him to accept money in Volodarka and to allow all of the Stavisht Jews to return home.

The bridge between Volodarka and Stavisht was broken, so they built a makeshift bridge and my grandfather stood by until the last of the Stavisht Jews had passed, then he and his family went home.

After many similar experiences, my grandfather, my grandmother and his family decided to flee to Romania. They then went to London and in 1928, they came to America.

[Page 59/60]

My Grandfather

by Arel, grandson of Eliyahu Shohet

When I started to read Yiddish literature in America, I discovered words and phrases written by Jewish classical writers, especially Mendele and Sholem Aleichem, which were familiar to me. I had heard them in my childhood from my grandfather, Rabbi Eliyahu Shohet, or as they used to call him in Stavisht, Elye Velvl Khaves. My grandfather, may his memory be for a blessing, did not read Yiddish literature, but I am certain that if he had been born and had lived under different circumstances he would have become a brilliant artist or writer.

He was skilled in telling a story with colorful descriptions, not only of the characters in the story, but also of the surroundings, of nature. If the story was set in a forest, he described the trees in glorious color. I later encountered in literature the folk sayings and proverbs that he used.

My first memory of my grandfather is when I was five years old. I remember how he wrapped me in a prayer shawl and carried me to Yosl Zyames to study the alef beys [Hebrew alphabet]. Along the way he told me a wonderful story in his inimitable fashion. "My child," he began, "I am carrying you now to enter upon the study of Torah. You knew the subject well, before you were born. Beside every Jewish child in his mother's womb there sits an angel who studies Torah with him for Torah is the foundation of the Jewish people. But just as soon as the child is born the angel taps him below the nostrils and he forgets everything he has learned so far. It appears that those up above do not want it to be too easy for Jews. So, the child is told: 'Go and study! Study Torah, that is your calling. Only in this way will you be different from other nations.'" To prove the truth of his story, my grandfather showed me the cleft on my upper lip below the nostrils. "This is the sign of the tap the angel gave you," he said.

Eliahu Shohet, his wife Feyge, and their daughter Pesi

This story moved me to come to my grandfather's every Friday night. Saturday morning, while I was still in bed, he would tell me some of his wonderful stories which I drank in thirstily.

It is from my grandfather that I inherited my great love for Jewish literature, novels and poetry. My grandfather also loved music very much. His house was not far from the Catholic church and although he was a pious Jew, as were all Jews in town, he used to walk with me on a Sunday, so that no one would see us, to the entrance of the Church to hear the organ music. He told me how the prophets [sic! the priests] sang and played instruments in the Holy Temple. He told me about this with such awesome descriptions as if he himself had been there. Then we would go to the tree lined streets of the Count's estate and he would show me the gardens and the flowers and the peacocks all the while continuing to tell me beautiful stories.

Dear Grandfather! I cannot thank you now for the dear words you planted within me and the love for my people and its literature. May these few words serve as a monument to your memory.

The founder and first president of the Stavisht Society in New York
Tsadok (Charles) Mazer, of blessed memory

[Page 63/64]

My Parents

by Aharon Shohet (Arthur Schechter)

My father, Meir, Elye Velvl Khaves was my grandfather Elye's only son. He had more modern traits, he was more practical. I was more closely nurtured by my grandfather in my childhood than by my father.

I got to know my father better in America. He came in 1921 and died in 1945. I remember my father more as the one who supported his family, his wife and seven or eight children, a very difficult task in those years. I was the oldest son to whom one could express the burdens of life of that time. For example: Who are your friends, what will become of you, you are already eleven years old and you are not studying hard, your friends are not of your class, unless you want to become, God forbid, an artisan.

These warnings did not frighten me. I had a weakness for artisans, tailors and especially seamstresses. I would often go to help them write letters to their fathers, and possibly boyfriends, in America. I would stay for hours and hear them sing their sad songs which we did not hear in middle-class homes. [He is referring here to a whole genre of songs about love betrayed.] I would sometimes spend whole days there. Naturally, I would get my reward for this from my father. The worst problems, however, were on Tuesdays, the day of the famous Stavisht fair. I was drawn to the fair as if by magnets, to the panorama of people: peasants with their sons and daughters, dressed in brightly embroidered clothing, with their horses, oxen, and sheep to sell. The colorful stands with the cakes on display and especially the beggars with their lyres singing doleful songs in a minor key which touched my heart.

Who could sit in a classroom and look at a careworn teacher on such a day? I imagined that he, too, would have preferred to do business in the market and get rid of his class full of reluctant students for a few hours.

After I was twelve years old, my father decided that he would no longer pay tuition for me, possibly because he could not afford to. There were six younger children for whom he had to provide.

Meir and Hanna Shohet

I would recall here a story about our rabbi, Rabbi Yaakov-Yosef: he had two sons about my age, Hershl and Moti. Hershl was a very good student. Moti was a dreamer, like me, and not a good student, and since he also did not go to heder, we decided to study together in his house. One day the rabbi came in and found Moti and me sitting at the table with a book. He asked me, "What are you doing here, my lad?" I answered, "I am studying with Moti." He smiled and said, "No you are not studying. If you really wanted to learn something, you would study with Hershl."

Nevertheless, I did learn something. I also experienced my parents' love for me when I left for America, alone, at age fourteen. I stubbornly insisted that I wanted to go into the wide world. I cannot forget their tears and their wishes: "Remain a Jew, my child, remember that we, your parents, raised you in the Jewish spirit. Do not break the thread, God forbid!" It seems to me, my parents, that I have fulfilled your wish.

I want to mention my uncle whose name is in the list of those killed in the Stavisht pogroms. His name was Shalom, he was called Shalom Denis in Stavisht. His home was near Gedalkes Lake among the gentiles. Jews hid there until my uncle became very ill. Most of the Jews had fled, but he remained because he was so sick. A small gang of bandits came in and cut off his head. May his soul be bound up in the bonds of eternal life. He had no children, but he loved all children, especially his nephews. We brought his wife, Aunt Sheyndl, to America and she died in Boston in the thirties.

I should also like to mention my father's cousin, Simha Shohet. He resembled my father as much as if he were his brother, although his character was very different. His daughter, Ita Shohet-Vaysman, died in Tel Aviv about four years ago. I met her in 1949, after forty years, and she inspired me with her wit and wisdom. I was also inspired by her husband, writer A. Vaysman, editor of this book, and their lovely children.

[Page 67/68]

I Visit My Grandfather

by Hava Goldman
Hebron, Connecticut

This happened when I was a very young girl, almost fifty years ago. My brother Moshe, Professor Moshe Haysinski of the Madam Curie Laboratory in Paris, was brought up in Stavisht at the home of my grandfather, Rabbi Yitshak Avraham Gaysinski.

I used to go from my hometown of Tarashcha to my grandparents every holiday. I used to go with Yona the waggoner in an open carriage with his three good horses. Once, on a holiday eve just as we left Tarashcha, a cold rain began to fall and became stronger and stronger, almost a flood. The horses kept stopping, not wanting to continue, and Yona did not spare the whip. The carriage had to stop. The horses could no longer find their way because of the rain.

The journey that ordinarily took three hours lasted five and when we finally arrived in Stavisht it was dark. The holiday candles shone from every home. All the households were in the synagogues and Yona had a problem. How can he bring his carriage to the Sokolovka synagogue and how can I, the grandchild of a rabbi, appear with my valise on a holiday? In those days no one would dare travel in town with a horse and carriage on Sabbath or holidays. Yona remembered that a friend of mine, Devora Sigal, lived not far from the outskirts of town, so he left me off at her house. When I knocked on her door, I was taken in and received warmly. They took off my wet clothing and sat me up over the oven, dressed me in dry clothing and gave me a holiday meal. There was no telephone in town in those days and only on the morrow when Devora's brother, I think his name was Motl, went to the synagogue, he said that I had spent the night at his home and someone came to take me to my grandparents.

If any of the Sigals read these lines, I want them to know that I am thankful for their friendship.

For some days the memory of my trip in the rain was frightening, but since it was Sukkot the joy of the holiday soon erased the frightening memory. Every morning, Yosl the beadle would bring the etrog [citron] and lulav [palm leaves bound with willow and myrtle branches] for us to say the blessing. We ate in the sukkah [booth] all week long. On Simhat Torah we went to the Sokolovka Kloyz, prayed, walked around with the Torah scrolls, sang and danced. On Simhat Torah in the daytime, all the householders of the Sokolovka Kloyz came to my grandfather's, made Kiddush [blessing on wine], then ate the holiday goodies provided by my grandmother. They sang and danced without cease.

I remember some of my grandfather's friends: Yekl Hirsh Reuvens, Mekhl Elushes, the Alanovskis, and many more whose names I no longer remember. I remember the old cantor Ya'akov-Yisrael, as soon as he started to sing he would begin to cough. It would take him a long time to recover from his coughing spell and continue singing.

When I recall those days I feel as if a great part of Jewish life and tradition is gone. It will take a long time before American Jewry returns to the old time Yidishkayt. Let us hope that they will return, because without Yidishkayt, without Jewish rejoicing, life is bleak.

[Page 71/72]

Impressions

by Yisrael Rubin
New York, New York

Yisrael Rubin

My name in Stavisht was Yisrolik Robtshanski, the son of Yehoshua the butcher. I was an apothecary and had a drugstore. I am now writing about the period of the First World War and the Russian Revolution which followed soon after. I opened my business in the middle of the war in a new building in the town center. It was owned by Mordekhai Tetievski, the son of Moshe Tetievski. The building had two stories. Downstairs Nisan Ayzenshteyn and his wife Tabl lived. He was the son-in-law of Pinhas Shpalski who had a tobacco store where he lived. I lived and had my store on the second story.

Mordekhai Tetievski had a brother-in-law, Fayvel Polyak, who lived in a nearby house. When Nisan Ayzenshteyn, Fayvel Polyak and my brother Fayvel were called to serve in the military, they all decided not to go.

It was a dangerous time. The majority of those who went to war did not return. Only a small minority returned, sick and crippled. Therefore, the three of them decided to hide out for as long as they could. They dug a hole under the building and made a room with an entrance from everyone's window and when there was a search out for them in town they would go into the hole and hide there until the search was over and then they would return home. My brother Fayvel stayed with me.

The searches were carried on quite frequently. Special agents would come from the district capital in Tarashcha to search for recruits and every time they would find 40-50 young men and they would also arrest the people who had hidden them. They used to come to our home, too, but fortunately never found anyone. This lasted for 18 months. The Russian Revolution occurred in August 1917. On that Simhat Torah, there was a great fright because the official came from Tarashcha with over 100 officers to carry out a house-to-house search. That night they found and arrested 75-80 people. The whole time they were in town there was great fear. No one would step out of his house until they left.

[Page 73-74]

**Yosef Rubin (Rabtshanski) with his family, below in middle:
Yehosua and his wife Iziye; top right: Avraham; top left: Binyamin;
below right: Shelomo; below left: Moshe. [We assume that the top
center photo of the man with the beard is Yosef Rubin, although it is
not in the text.] Yosef Rubtshanski and his wife Batya were killed
by the Zelianevtsi band of murderers in 1920.**

[*Translators note*: the variant spellings of the name Rabtshanski and Rubtshanski
appear in the same caption!]

After the Revolution our three young men decided to join the army. They served for a short period of time and came home safe and sound. But new troubles began, both on the part of the ever-changing government and the gangs of bandits who roamed around. Every time there was a change of regime a new gang of bandits would come in and they would leave death and destruction behind, robbing, stealing, burning, and killing. First came the Germans, then the Petliures, Denikins, Zelenys, Gregorovitses, and then the Bolsheviks.

This lasted for almost two years with not one day of peace and quiet. One fine day our family decided to leave everything behind, business, houses, property, and to go to Shvarts Timeh [black uncleanliness, the Yiddish nickname for Belaya Tserkov, white church, also called in Hebrew Sede Lavan, white field.] I, my parents, and the children were there for a short time. I left for Kiev where I lived on Bolshoi Podvalnye and worked as a pharmacist in a Bolshevik apothecary in Lukianovski prison for almost a year. When I received a few days leave I went to Shvarts Timeh to see my parents. We had a long discussion and decided to leave for America. This was May 1919.

Four families left, my parents with their children, two uncles with their families, and my family. It took a lot longer than it takes to tell. First I went back to Kiev. We decided that when they would be prepared to leave, they would let me know and we would go together to the Romanian border.

After a short while they let me know that they were ready to leave on a certain day. I got a month's vacation and prepared to leave. We immediately went to Zegivke, a small town near the border of Bessarabia, then part of Romania. We were unable to cross the border all together. Each family crossed separately; first, the younger children, then the older folk. We were in Kishinev, Bessarabia for eight months.

We tried to get money and papers from America. We managed to settle in nicely in Kishinev, each family in its own profession and we made a good living. The first three months we were there I worked in the Ukrainian committee, then I worked as an apothecary for a year and then as a cashier and bookkeeper in a large haberdashery store for 15 months. We spent 2 ½ years in Romania, the last three months in Bucharest waiting for the visas and money.

We did not go to America all together. Whoever received a visa left immediately. In four months time all the families had arrived in America. My parents came later, after 1923 when the quota for Russian immigrants was closed. We settled in well in America and we all make a living, and we thank God who inspired us to leave the Bolshevik claws and the damned Russian murderers behind the iron curtain.

[Page 77/78]

From Stavisht to America

by M. Galant
New York, New York

M. Galant

Stavisht, Kiev Province where I spent part of my life, was blessed by nature with an unusual panorama: on all sides of the town there were high mountains, trees, and rivers. All the roads leading into town were bordered by 100 year old pine and poplar trees, mainly on the side of the Count's estate (Stavisht belonged to Count Branicki).

One could be enchanted by the air and the beauty of the castles, gardens with tree-lined streets and flowers. Under the trees there were benches. The residents used to promenade there on Sabbaths and holidays and in the summer evenings, breathing the fresh air. The town itself was dirty. There were no street cleaners and the wind carried the dust aloft. The rains would clean the narrow streets and the large empty places somewhat.

Stavisht had many merchants, few artisans, and many waggoners for it was far from a train station and the district capital of Tarashcha, and 18-20 viorst [slightly longer than a kilometer] from the sugar factory of Zhashkov with which it was commercially connected.

We also had plenty of idlers, with little sticks in their hands, looking for a way to earn money as agents.

Stavisht was the headquarters of Count Branicki's estates and there were many of his Polish officials there who were good customers in the Jewish shops. However, in the last years, the Count's estate had set up a large cooperative store and the Jewish shopkeepers suffered.

But Stavisht Jews were not pessimists. Far from rich, but always lively and merry. Stavisht was famous for its cracklings. "Stavishter grivn" were known in all of the villages in the area. [Cracklings, non-kosher, are roast pork skin. Kosher cracklings are fried chicken skin, chicken fat, and onions. Can also be goose or duck.]

Stavisht did not have a place in Jewish cultural life. Its people were pious and fanatic and the children were raised in that spirit. The heder played an important role, first on the elementary level, and then after two or three years, with a teacher of higher learning. But the heder of Shemuel Krentsel, "Shemuel the Melamed" [teacher of young children], was different. He was not Orthodox. He taught in a modern style. Everyday a teacher would come in for 2-3 hours to teach Russian studies. For a while it was Sigal, or the writer of these lines.

There were two well-known modern teachers in Stavisht: Yisrael Tsinis (now in Israel) and Lozer Yarmolinski. Their students were 12-13 years old, had already acquired some knowledge and had a different outlook at the world.

As I remember on the highest hill, the Vitrak, on the way to Zhashkov, there was a Russian School with four classes of gymnasium (but no foreign languages) which Jewish children were forbidden to attend. In 1909 Jewish children were allowed to take the examination. I prepared nine children of whom eight passed the exam, and from that time Jewish students were allowed in with the *numerus clausus* [quota for Jews].

At Reuven Yagovski's there was a "little bank" which a group of merchants had founded to help needy people with loans. Later the government gave permission to open a legal credit union under the direction of Efrayim Mazur whom everybody in town respected.

I still remember when there was no post or telegraph office in Stavisht. Old Mendl the Lame would sometimes bring someone a letter. Somewhat later a post and telegraph office was opened in Aharon Duaduak's house. Then it was transferred to a larger house, that of Mordekhai Sukanik. Stavisht flourished. A mailman appeared in the streets who stopped bypassers and asked them where various people lived. People began subscribing to journals and our town was involved in correspondence.

When the Zionist movement began in Russia our townspeople became quite worldly. I don't remember who founded the Zionist organization in Stavisht, builders of the "Zionist Kloyz."

The Jews of Stavisht were always peaceful and friendly and constantly hoped that better times would come. Came the Russian Revolution and we rejoiced. But the joy did not last very long. All over Ukraine pogroms against Jews broke out and the wild bands did not overlook our town. Jewish blood was spilled. Old and young were murdered. We were robbed of our possessions. The Jews of Stavisht, like the Jews of all of the small towns, fled to all ends of the earth.

As you know, Stavisht belonged to Count Branicki. All the Jewish homes were on his property. We paid rent. If anybody wanted to build an outhouse for hygienic reasons, he could not because it was not in the contract. We Jews did not have much pleasure from the Count. He had no Jewish officials. At one time Leyzer Rubtshinski had served as an official and a family named Shkod, an old man and two sons, had supervised the distillery where liquor was produced, but then they were all fired. Only two Jews remained on the Count's estate: Aizik Landa and Shemuel Postrelke, a bookbinder.

You know the old saying, "If you need the thief, you take him off the gallows." For a short time the Count's estate provided a little stove in the women's gallery of the Bet Hamidrash and every Sabbath a gentile would come and light it so that we had fresh tea – but it lasted only a few months.

Who does not remember Mendl-Ber and his kapelye [orchestra] who made merry for our weddings? In the summertime the weddings were held in the wooden hut. The members of the wedding used to dance on the sand. But Mendl-Ber left Stavisht. The kapelye was divided. One part had a famous fiddle player, Gadzenke from Skvira, and they got the upper hand. There were clashes between the two groups every time they met. I remember once, Hanukkah time, my mother reminded me to say my prayers and not forget "al hanisim" [said on the holiday]. After I finished I went out. I heard terrible cries. I ran toward the sounds and what did I see? The two parts of this band who used to play together so merrily were exchanging blows with sticks. Their playing was no longer so merry. The police arrested them all, but it seems that our jail was too crowded, so they were all set free.

Sensational Events

There was a sensational event in Stavisht when Nehama Kleynman the daughter of a lawyer, a graceful and beautiful girl, fell in love with a musician. Her parents were opposed to the match and Nehama suffered, but one fine morning she and her lover eloped. They were pursued but not found. They went to his parents, got married, and left for America.

The second sensation was caused by my close friend, xxx [name blacked out in book after it was printed.] It seems he could not find a pretty girl to love, so he had an affair with a married woman, the mother of two. When the husband discovered the goings on he came to a compromise with xxx. He gave him the woman and a son, xxx's, and he took his own two children.

Moshe was the waggoner who took passengers to Tarashcha. His nickname was "Gehenna" [hell]. The waggoner who went to Zhashkov was Avraham'ke, nicknamed "The world to come." Among the many waggoners who went to Belaya Tserkov ("Shvarts Timeh") there was one called "Moshe Kishke" [guts]. There was only one without a nickname, but everybody in Stavisht, young and old, knew him. That was Yankl (Ya'akov) Dantsis. As soon as he came to the station square you could hear his resounding voice. Everyone knew Yankl Dantsis' voice. As Sholem Aleichem [might have] said, "There was only one Yankl Dantsis." No one in town had ever heard about his good deeds. He would often be escorted by a convoy from Stavisht to Tarashcha. His escorts would be relieved in the village of Yasinovke, where my in-laws lived. They would give him something to eat so that he would have the strength to continue on the next lap of his journey.

Brief Profiles

Leyb Trembitski was a famous medical professor. In America people are accustomed to using the familiar form "du" [you, singular] rather than the polite "ir" [you, plural]. Trembitski always said "we." It seems that he had a lot of doctors in his pocket. Once, two doctors, Garakh and Milevski, complained to him that they were not well. He replied, "Search for health in the bowl."

There was a woman named Batya Rasis who had a general store where you could find everything. Her husband, Ya'akov Rabinovitsh, spent more time in the synagogue than in the store. She ruled the roost, was the leading woman in town, and everyone loved her. She was clever and could tell stories and, when Wolf the tailor, who had one blind eye, came in, then you would really hear some storytelling…

Pitsie Sheynes was always smartly dressed even Count Branicki could not vie with him. He had big beautiful shoes that were really outstanding. If you asked how much his shoes cost, he would only tell you how much one shoe cost.

There was also Shelomo the tailor, a quiet upstanding man. His son Yokl (Jack) was very kind to me when I came to America. I don't know if the most pious man in Stavisht would have done as much to help someone.

[Page 85/86]

What I Remember About Stavisht

by Meir Spektor
Tel Aviv, Israel

The name of the town was spelled Stavishtshe. In Russian that means ponds because the town was surrounded by ponds on three sides. More accurately we should call them lakes, large wide lakes which teemed with delicious fish. There were carp, perch, and other kinds of fish which provided tasty meals for the holy Sabbath feasts.

There were the sandy ponds, around which were the clay fields where the white and tallow clay was dug up for whitewashing the walls and for smoothing on the kitchen floors Sabbath eve.

There was the brick pond whose clay was suitable for making bricks. I do not know whether or not it was used for this purpose.

There was a bath pond, near which stood the old Jewish bathhouse.

The town belonged to Count Branicki, a famous wealthy Polish magnate. The story was told about him that he owned one thousand estates. He sold one so that people would have to say "nine hundred and ninety nine" instead of just the one word "thousand."

A highway divided the town into two parts. It started at the Count's palaces where his officials lived. They were all Poles, of course. Many of the Stavisht merchants learned how to speak Polish for that reason.

The palaces stood among thick orchards and gardens where there were all kinds of fruit and flowers. From the estate to the first Jewish houses there was a "boulevard," a narrow strip of land bordered by small wooden columns and tall trees and dense lilac bushes whose fragrance, especially during the month of May, was heavenly. Next to the trees were benches. The promenaders, especially we youth, would sit there for hours on quiet moonlit nights until the break of dawn. It was a pleasure to sit there at night in the quiet when the breeze would intoxicate us with the fragrance of the flowers and the pine trees. From the woods we would hear the sweet trill of the larks. Sitting with you, leaning on your shoulder, is a dark-haired or blonde girl, and you are young and carefree.

I shall never forget the Friday and Sabbath nights.

On the other side of the sandy pond, going to the right towards Zhashkov, was the thick pine forest which stretched for hundreds of viorst. During the summers groups of boys and girls would stroll among the fragrant pines. The forest was so thick the rays of sunlight could not penetrate. We would pick sweet berries and dash through the forest yelling, "Ooha, ooha!" just to hear the mysterious other-worldly echo reply. That is how we would spend our Sabbath afternoons until nightfall and end the evening on the boulevard under the trees, not alone, you understand…

The town had a number of twisting streets and many alleys. In the middle of town was the highway paved with cobblestones. When you walked there in the summertime, you could twist your ankles on the cobblestones. In the wintertime, before Passover when the snow started to melt, you walked in mud over your ankles. Nevertheless, you always tried to walk on the highway because the mud on the sides was so thick you could lose your shoes and galoshes in it.

The highway started at the Count's estate, the road to "Shvarts Timeh" [Belaya Tserkov], and continued downhill to the Count's mill by the brick pond. From there it continued on to Uman. On the left, uphill from the bath pond, there was the road to Tarashcha, the district capital.

The name given to the pond, "bath pond," was because of the old bathhouse at its edge. There were the wooden outhouses where on the hot summer afternoons the householders of the nearby streets and especially the school boys would often run to "take care of matters" or just to get away from the teacher and the difficult Talmud lesson. Often the schoolrooms would empty out on hot days.

While the students were enjoying themselves at the pond, the teacher would catch a snooze and dream about the Holy Land. Most of the teachers in town were fervent Zionists and dreamt about Erets Yisrael. My teacher, Rabbi Yisrael Shumsky, or as he was nicknamed, "Yisrolik the melamed" or "Yisrael Tsines" has been living in Erets Yisrael for quite a long time.

Even though the town was quite small, it had a number of small prayer houses and the large old wooden synagogue. The school boys would shiver when they walked past it on dark winter nights, carrying their lanterns, for they feared the dead who would arise in the night to pray there.

The "Makarov Kloyz" and the "big Bet Hamidrash" were where the elite went to pray. Nevertheless, if someone did not get the honors he felt due him, there could be quarreling and even candelabra flying from the pulpit towards the heads of the offenders.

The more respectable householders lived on both sides of the highway: merchants, shopkeepers, wealthy dealers in grain. The simple folk lived along the alleys behind.

On Synagogue Street and surrounding streets lived the artisans: tailors, cobblers, carpenters, butchers, and waggoners. On the bath street in small humpbacked wooded shacks with straw roofs, lived the poorest class: tar makers, rope makers, peddlers who spent their weekdays traveling from one gentile village to another trying to make a living, and just plain paupers.

People did not use surnames in Stavisht. Everyone was called by a father's or grandfather's or wife's name. Sometimes a nickname was given for the color of one's beard. Thus, for example, there were two Yoeliks, both fine men, owners of dry-goods stores. One was called "Yoelik the black" because he had a fine respectable black beard and the other was called "Yoelik the red" because of his red beard. My grandfather was called "Arye Meir Dina's" for both his grandfather and grandmother. My mother's brother, my uncle Fishl, was called "Fishl Moshe Yosi's" and my mother was called "Shifra Moshe Yosi's." My uncle Pesah Hersh Salganik was called "Pesah Hersh Trayne's" for his wife's name was Trayne, and his son was called "Shmulik Pesah Hersh's," but his older son was called Shelomo Salganik. Why? Because his fine foods shop stood removed from the other shops in town and was patronized only by the nobles from the Count's estate. Also he socialized with Simha Shohet and Barukh Boyarski and played chess and even cards with them. [Spector explains the way the names are formed and he does use apostrophes.]

There were a handful of householders, important grain dealers, who frequented the Count's estate, and government officials who spent their time mostly in the big cities. They were called by their family names, e.g. Simha Shohet, Barukh Boyarski, Granovski, etc.

There were quite a few waggoners in town. They transported the shopkeepers to Shvarts Timeh and Berditshev to buy goods. They would sit in the wagon on pallets of straw covered with straw mats.

There were two waggoners who were nicknamed "Garden of Eden" and "Gehenna." "Garden of Eden" went to Zhashkov and "Gehenna" went to Tarashcha. "Garden of Eden" was a tall heavy man with a black beard, a good natured smiling face, and with a chuckle would call out "Nu, children, crawl, you should excuse the expression, into the wagon."

"Gehenna" was a mean-spirited blonde man always angry at the world. He never uttered a kind word. He addressed everyone, young and old, by the familiar "du." "Why are you standing there like a golem [in Jewish folklore, a clay creature magically brought to life]? Are you waiting for respect or your inheritance? And maybe you'll throw yourself into the wagon already?"

There were water carriers, blacksmiths, large heavy-set men with thick black beards covering their faces, always wearing high heavy boots smeared with pitch, simple folk, weak in Hebrew, who would kill themselves for an aliyah in kloyz, but they were all good hearty Jews.

On the other side of the sand pond on the road to Zhashkov, on the hill which went down to the waterside, was the cemetery, overgrown with thorny and burry bushes. The wooden slats of the wall surrounding it were broken and falling apart, the old wooden markers were crooked, fallen and covered with the green moss of generations, the letters rubbed out. But the relatives of the dead knew where their burial places were from the mementos they left behind at every visit.

On Tisha B'Av [ninth of Av, a fast day] and Rosh Hodesh [first day of the month] all the inhabitants of the town would come to visit the graves, to ask for help for the living. Meanwhile, the boys would collect burrs which they would then throw at one another in the synagogue during the reading of kines [Book of Lamentations and other lamentations read during the Ninth of Av].

At the border of the Count's estate stood the Russian Orthodox church. There the gentiles of the neighboring villages and farms would gather on Sundays and Christian holidays. They would leave their wagons in the marketplace, from the church up to the Jewish shops, unhitching their horses and tying them up behind the wagons, and then, families in tow, would wend their way to the church to hear the priest preach.

After the prayer service the gentile families would come to the marketplace and go shopping in the Jewish stores which stood in two long rows, built of wooden weather-beaten boards. Sunday was market day, almost a fair. The gentiles would buy everything beginning with an "A" [e.g. a shirt, a spool of thread, etc.] and the Jews earned a living from the gentiles. In general, the local gentiles and the Jews got along on a friendly basis.

There were frequent fights after the men had drunk a great deal in the "Monopol" [government monopoly of liquor] near the whiskey shop, but the old town policeman, Sergei, would quickly make peace. He would cuss out the "Russian Orthodox people," who laughed at him, and beat some of them with his club. Then they would once more crowd into the Jewish inns to drink and eat some good food, and Jews would again, thank God, earn some money.

The weekly fair took place on Tuesdays. Thousands of gentiles would come in their wagons to wheel and deal. They would bring their produce to sell to the Jews and they would buy their household goods, material for a dress, a kerchief or a pair of pants, and boots for themselves and their children.

The town lay amidst ponds and forest and wide green fields surrounded by a sea of gentiles who had lived at peace with the Jews for many years. On the Jewish holidays the peasants would bring their Jewish friends gifts of produce from their orchards and gardens and fat fish from the river for the Sabbath. In the wintertime, for Christmas, they would come in the greatest frost and snow to bless their Jewish friends, pouring wheat and barley over them, as was the custom, and receiving in return halot [white loaves baked for the Sabbath. I use the Library of Congress transliteration for the Hebrew het. In England it is common to use ch.]

Who could imagine that these fine peasants would suddenly turn into cruel wild animals, dreadful murderers, who would kill their old friends and destroy the entire town which had never done them any wrong. It is written, "Do not depend upon human beings," or as Tevya the milkman explained, "Do not trust a gentile, even in his grave." The hatred of Jews lies deep in the gentile heart. As fine as exile is, it is still exile, not like being at home. We should thank God that we have lived to see a Jewish state, the State of Israel. Here we will not suffer from gentile "brotherliness." Here no gentile youth will set his dogs on Jewish boys, and here we will not hear the derogatory "Zhid" or "Sheeny."

[Page 95/96]

From My Childhood

by Yosl (Syuni) Golub
New York, New York

I remember my childhood years as if peering through a mist. I can see my first experiences, the wonderful beautful years in my sleepy little town, Stavisht, and then the nightmare changes, the horrible experiences of that time, the robberies and tortures and the burning of my little town of Stavisht.

I am still sorry that I was so young when we, together with hundreds of other residents, fled from Stavisht, and I did not experience any more of the golden days which filled my childhood.

Now, forty years later in the big city of New York, I recall the unforgettable scenes of childhood, as well as the bitter times, my last days and hours in Stavisht. When the rumors came that a new band that had destroyed and murdered all the inhabitants of Tetiyev was heading towards Stavisht, my parents grabbed the children and together with the rest of the inhabitants began to run along the road from the church to Belaya Tserkov. It was a long way. As I write these lines I relive the experience as if it had happened only yesterday.

From the church to the mill (from one end of town to the other) there was a highway lined with small pillars on both sides and telephone poles every four hundred feet. There were footpaths leading to the houses and shops which stood on both sides of the highway. In the middle of town were a few inns, the government bank, and the Bet Hamidrash.

The town had probably gotten its name from the Ukrainian word "Stav" which means lake. I imagine that the many lakes in Stavisht had something to do with its name. Here in America the town would have been called Lakeland or Lakeside or Lakeview.

The Jewish part of Stavisht started at the Catholic church and went from the boulevard, the town park on the right and left of the highway which divided the town into two parts all the way to the mill. On the right side after the church was the town pump where we got our water. From there the road led through the village of Raskashne to Zhashkov. This was also the road that led to the cemetery, to the government high school and also to the distillery.

On the right side of the highway, after the pump, there was an empty plaza. On fair days the gentiles would tie up their horses and wagons there and set out the products which they had brought with them to sell. They would also put up stands where they would set out their wares. Here onc could see pots, embroidered and knitted clothing, icons, and other village handiwork.

A little further down were the Jewish shops which sold manufactured goods, groceries, suits of clothing, and other items which village peasants could acquire only in town. A little further down, on the right hand side of the highway, there were butcher shops and a few fishmongers and some stores which sold flour, bread, and so on. Then came the bank, surrounded by a wooden fence. During the summertime the peasants would stand near the fence and sell fresh fruit, vegetables and berries.

On the left hand side of the highway across from the church was the police station with its few officers. Behind Yagovski's apothecary shop there was a gentile butcher shop that sold all kinds of sausages, pickled foods and conserves. Then came Smushkin's house and yard. Smushkin was the richest man in Stavisht. He had his own horses and wagons in his courtyard. A little further down were the inns. Here too were the establishments of Yankl Berdishevski, Yosl Grosman, Zelig Levinson, Gulba, Nehemiah the watchmaker, Hershl the maker of uppers for shoes, Reuven the tailor's inn courtyard, Solomon Golub's book store and house, Tetievski's inn courtyard, Potovski's inn courtyard, Rubtshanski's apothecary shop, Noah Wilfand's house and the Beth Hamidrash.

On both sides of the highway, on the way to the mill, there were many houses standing in a row. Others were scattered about and among them a shop or a business. On the left side there was a house with a large porch, then came Alter Baltyanski's grocery store and the Talnoye Kloyz. A little further from the highway, it seems to me, was Golditshe's house with the only telephone in Stavisht. Lower down were Binyamin Feinzilberg's apothecary shop, Dadyuk's house where the Hefets family lived, and further down was the town hall, where from time to time there was an exhibition or a film. Here I saw a film for the first time in my life, "The Exodus from Egypt." Somewhere around here was the only photographer in Stavisht, Haym Leyb's inn courtyard, the Glants family lived there. Further down lived the Bisitski, Persyan, and Boyarski families and right at the edge of town, it seems to me, was the town apothecary shop. On the right hand side of the highway lived the Wilfand family – Yank and Sonia and their parents, and right next to them was the Makarov Kloyz and then came some houses whose owners I do not remember. I do remember the house of Shmuel Krentsel (the melamed). Then came the home of the dentist, Luzya the melamed's house, the Zaslavsky printing shop on a hill, the Marynovski house, the church, and further down I remember was a blacksmith, Yankl the blacksmith, it seems to me. Then came Gedalke's lake and then the mill. From here there was a road through the hillside to the tarelke [the word means saucer or bowl, it may have been a local name for a basin-like area] and to Tarashcha.

Between Golub's and Tetievski's houses there was an alleyway that led to the synagogue and Synagogue Street. The synagogue was a tall red wooden building, the tallest in town, it seems to me. On Synagogue Street lived the Fishlin family, Pitsie Sheyne's, the Golditsh family and Zelig Levinson, among others. Synagogue Street led to Feldsher [paramedic] Trembitski's house and also to the Pshinke, the gentile villages.

After the Bet Hamidrash there was a little street that turned left and led to the rabbi's house, to the Sokolovka Kloyz and right to Barukh Zeyger's house, to the Postrelkes, and to the neighborhood where stood the little house of my first teacher, Moshke Vaysman. Exactly opposite was a heder. Then, going downhill, there was the bathhouse and the town bathhouse — but this, it seems to me, was already outside the town limits.

Shemulik Beraza
Shelomo Golub's father-in-law

On the other side of the highway from the Bet Hamidrash and on the right hand side of the town bank was a street which led to the Zionist Kloyz. Nearby was the Jewish gymnasium and many houses, among them Mendl Ganapolski's house, and, it seems to me, the Horovits house, Yisrael Tsinis' house, Aynbinder, Tsherpovadski, and Hersh Mendl Shadkhen's house.

There were wider and narrower streets with houses on both sides of the highway. There lived the shopkeepers, tradesmen, and artisans –tailors, seamstresses, cobblers, hat makers, carpenters, coopers, tinsmiths, waggoners, porters, blacksmiths, and so on and so on.

Up from the church the highway went past the Count's estate and there were princely dwellings on both sides, then Doctor Garakh and the town judge with their fine houses and large gardens and the town hospital. Then the road led past villages, large and small, through fields and woods towards Belaya Tserkov (Shvarts Timeh) the largest city on the way to Kiev. It used to take a whole day and night to get there with a horse and wagon.

I remember the footpath from the highway to our house and to my father's book store. There were steps leading up to the porch and then one entered the store. We sold all kinds of articles in our book store. One could buy musical instruments, gramaphones, records, sewing kits, pen knives, cosmetics, candies, conserves, etc.

All of the town's gentile intellectuals, teachers and students, nobles and peasants, all found what they needed in my father's store. We even received the newspapers from Kiev.

Our Jewish customers bought Yiddish and Hebrew books, prayer books, and other Jewish ritual articles.

Our dwelling was in the same building as our store. We had about four or five rooms. One of the rooms had a stove which was heated in the wintertime with sheaves of straw. The stove provided warmth for the entire house. There was a large oven in the kitchen. It was a pleasure to lie on the shelf over the oven in the wintertime. That is why I loved the kitchen most of all. First of all, the fine odors of delicious food came from the kitchen where my mother and the maidservant cooked. When they baked bread or rendered fat the smells would permeate the entire house. The fragrance of cracklings, and of borsht, remains with me to this day. There were usually a few guests in my mother's kitchen, Yosi Mazerake, Itsikel the madman, or other poor people invited by my mother to partake of a meal.

There was a door from the kitchen to the storeroom, a large room full of logs for wintertime. Here too was the water barrel for household use, as well as barrels of sauerkraut, pickles and sour apples. From this room a ladder went up to the attic. There, hanging from the ceiling, were dried fruits. Under a straw cover were fresh apples and pears. That is why the attic had the most delightful smells. I would go up to the attic from time to time to enjoy the aromas, as well as the heavenly tastes.

There was a door from the storeroom which led to Synagogue Street. At the side was a door to the courtyard of our neighbor, Reuven the tailor. The courtyard was a large enclosed space with a high roof. Quite often peasants and waggoners or simple merchants would come to stay there for a few days and nights. There was a smell of horses and straw there. In the summertime my mother and her neighbors, Hayah Shakhanovitsh and Beyle Dorf, would make jams there on large brass trays. For us children this was a very important occasion and the taste of the jam has remained with me to this day.

Between our house and Tetievski's inn courtyard was a little street which led to Synagogue Street. In the middle of the street was a puddle which never dried up. Quite often, in the summertime and especially in the wintertime, horses and wagons would get stuck in it and not be able to get out. We could look out of a window of our house and see the horse and wagon stuck in the mud puddle. Sometimes it was Yankl Dantsis, the waggoner, or Velvl the porter. We children would run and look on. I cannot understand to this day why the people of Stavisht did not drain this puddle as well as the other mud holes which were abundant all over town.

I remember the twilight hours in Stavisht when the gentile boys would drive the herds of cattle home from the pastures. We could hear the boys and girls singing on their way home after a day's work in the beet fields. Their singing could be heard throughout the town until it was dark and quiet all around. We used to sit on our porch and listen. The barking of dogs would disturb the quiet of the night. From the ponds we would hear the croaking of the frogs. When the moon was out it would light up all of Stavisht. It seemed to us that our footpath leading to the highway was also a path to the moon. The roads from our town led to a wide unknown world. But the center of the unknown world was certainly my little town of Stavisht. The highway and the footpath led directly to my house, otherwise the moon would not have shone directly over us.

We used to fetch our water from the town pump near the church or from the few wells in town. And it seems to me that we also had a water carrier who would sell water from a large barrel on a wagon. One could hire a gentile boy or girl to bring water. At the pump one had to turn a large wheel in order to bring up the water. The water was very cold both in summer and winter. At the wells, one would lower a bucket with a rope, fill it with water, and draw it back up. Then the water would be carried home in two buckets attached to a wooden yoke which hung over one's shoulders. For most of the residents it was a long walk. But this was one of the acceptable discomforts of living in Stavisht. It was interesting to see the water carriers carry the water buckets without spilling even one drop of wter. This was a learned skill. Some of the water carriers did not even hold on to the yokes with their hands when they delivered water to the houses. When I was a young boy I viewed this as a heroic feat and wished to grow big so that I, too, could carry a yoke with two water buckets and not hold the yoke with my hands.

One of the local characters I remember was Stefan Visotski. He was a tall, well-built peasant with lots of black hair. All year long he wore a tall black hat. In the summertime he sold melons across from our house on the other side of the highway. He would build a little shed to protect his melons and sleep there at night. From our house we could see the lanterns which lit up Stefan and his melons. When Stefan got drunk he would forget about his melons and he would roll in the mud crying or singing, unrecognizable, covered with mud. But his melons were famous in town. Each melon squeaked when you held it in your hands.

I still regret the fact that my parents did not send me and my older brother Yani to a heder where all the Stavisht boys studied. Instead we had a private tutor, Moshke Vaysberg. I have nothing against him, but I would rather have gone to heder with all the boys my age. Every time I passed by a heder and heard the boys sing out the phrases from the Pentateuch in unison, I would feel a pang of envy. I wanted to be one of them, just like everybody. When I finally started to go to the Talmud Torah I began to feel like part of the crowd. My teachers were, as I remember, Luzi the melamed, Tsherpovodski, Lande, and, it seems to me, Yisrael Tsinis. My Talmud Torah friends made me forget about heder. Among my friends were Yosl Wilfand, Avraham Zeyger, Avraham Baltyanski, Naftoli Dorf, Binyamin Ganapolski, Avraham Rubtshanski, and a son of Lande. We founded a children's club called "Nekhde Tsiyon" [Grandsons of Zion] and afterwards "Yalde Tsiyon" [Children of Zion]. We had meetings and read aloud and sang Hebrew songs. Our town enriched our childhood imaginations with its natural beatuy, its gardens, fields, wood, lakes and hills.

I really did envy the heder boys. In the wintertime, they would come home late at night and carry along lanterns to light the way so that they would not step into the Stavisht mud holes in the dark. It seemed to me that it was a heroic act to walk home at night by the light of a lantern. I also envied the boys their hard-soled boots with which they could slide on the frozen puddles, which could take your breath away. Oh, if only my parents would have allowed me to wear hard-soled boots, which the heder boys wore, how happy I would have been.

In the summertime the boys would go bathe in the lake or go to Synagogue Street where they and the gentile boys from the Pshinke would throw stones at each other. Sometimes they would go pick up wood chips or fruit in the police station garden.

There was a lot more to the holidays than simply going to the synagogue and breathing in the sanctity of the prayers. First of all, we did not have to go to heder or Talmud Torah. Every holiday had its own character. We would look forward to it all year long. Getting ready for Pesah, making the pots and pans kosher, helping father burn the unleavened bread, etc., the Seder with the Pesah foods, playing various games with nuts. There was no holiday like it for a young boy. Moreover, it was the beginning of springtime and everything in nature was revived.

Then came Shavu'ot, with delicious dairy food, and once again we played games with nuts. On Lag Be-Omer we would prepare our weapons. Our "cannon" was an old lock with a an old nail tied into it. We used to rub the powder off the tops of matches, pour it into the keyhole of the lock with the nail, and slam it against a wall. Its bang could be heard all over town. Sometimes we would celebrate Lag Be-Omer in the tarelke behind the town on the hill on the way to Tarashcha. Sometimes my close friends and I would celebrate Lag Be-Omer in Barukh Zeyger's or Lande's gardens.

And so, too, with the other holidays. We celebrated Hamishah Asar Bi-Shevat with carobs, figs, and dates which we got only once a year. The High Holidays were more serious. First of all, there was more prayer in the synagogue. Then, on Yom Kippur, we would vie with one another as to who could fast longer. On Sukkot and Simhat Torah we were revived. We would build a sukkah and sitting in a sukkah meant dwelling directly under the Divine Presence. In the Torah procession we would carry little blue and white flags with an apple and a lighted candle on top. We would carry and kiss the Torah scrolls. For Hanukkah we would prepare little cards, drawing the pictures ourselves, showing our skill at drawing. We would play cards and spin tops. Then we would get Hanukkah gelt and eat latkes. At Purim time we boys were the leaders with our noisemakers and whenever the name of Haman was mentioned we would fill the synagogue with noise. Then we would come home to a festive meal.

That is why we looked forward to every holiday with longing. During the whole year we were kept busy in school. In the wintertime we would slide on the ice on skates or on the hard soles of our boots. We also had wooden sleds with which we would slide downhill behind Zaslavski's house. At home the stoves would be heated with sheaves of straw and the smoke would pour out of the chimneys up to heaven. The frost burned outdoors. When you pulled a sled behind you the snow would squeak under the runners.

In the summertime the Jewish students who studied in the big cities would come home for summer vacation. My oldest borther, Isak, was among them. You cannot imagine how I looked up to these young men and women who were gymnasium students. We had a wonderful group of students from Stavisht, of whom I remember these: Gedalyah and Isak Lande, Hershl Gorovits, Itsi Shadkhen, Shakhne Shakhanovitsh, Hershl Bisidski, Leyb Kubernik, Mutsi Volodarski, Brayne Shadkhen, Riva Fishlin, Gitl Faynzilberg, Sonia Wilfand. They made a fine sight as they promenaded on the boulevard in their uniforms with the gold buttons and their caps with the gold or silver crests. I idolized them, for they came from the big cities beyond the horizon, from the great unknown world. I wanted to grow up very quickly so I, too, could achieve the role of secondary school student from Stavisht. Unfortunately, it was not fated to happen. I did not get to be a heder boy with a lantern and hard-soled boots, nor a gymnasium student returning home to Stavisht in a uniform with gold buttons.

But I did get to be something of a secondary school student, without a uniform, but with a cap with a Hebrew crest. My father, with the help of a group of townspeople, founded a Hebrew secondary school in Stavisht. Their goal was to keep the young people at home, so they would not have to go far afield to study. They imported teachers from some distance, set up a physics laboratory, and so was founded the first Jewish secondary school in the area, in our Stavisht. All subjects were taught in Hebrew with Russian taught only as a language. It is impossible to evaluate what effect this institutuion had on our town. Unforutnately, we could not continue our studies for long. The dreadful events which came to pass soon put an end to this wonderful experiment, as they did to the lives of most of our townspeople.

Everyone in Stavisht was always busy trying to make a living, buying and selling, in handicrafts, etc. From time to time a cantor and choir would come from one of the big cities to appear in the big synagogue where the artisans prayed. We would listen to the chanting and derive great pleasure from it. I remember when the renowned Pinchik [Pierre S. Pinchik, 1887-1971] came and his sweet voice rose to the ceiling of the synagogue, if not higher. I envied the choristers. It was a great privilege for a boy to be a chorister, especially in the choir of a cantor like Pinchik.

On Fridays the shops would close earlier and business would cease. Then we would go to the bathhouse and afterwards, with slow measured steps, we would walk to evening prayers in the synagogue, the Bet Hamidrash, or to the Sokolovka, Talnoye, or Makarev Kloyz. My father and his three sons prayed in the Zionist Kloyz. It was quite a long walk from our house. We would walk down the highway then turn right at the bank. I especially loved these long walks. Sabbath reigned all around.

The Zionist Kloyz had the most comfortable and beautiful pews of any synagogue in town. When one faced the Holy Ark one really felt he was in God's house. The prayer leaders were, as I recall: Shiye Moshe, Yankl Salganik, Yankl Berditshevski, Yankl Shumski, and sometimes also Yisrael Tsinis. All of these men led the prayers at one time or another and it was a pleasure to hear their chanting, and of course, [it must have pleased] the Master of the Universe.

The Jews of Stavisht lived with faith. When the fair came everyone was busy with commerce, buying and selling, with lively noisy merriment. The peasants from the surrounding villages would come to town to sell their produce and they would wander around from store to store to buy what they needed. They would set up their wares in the marketplace next to their horses and wagons. There was not an empty place to be seen from one end of the marketplace to the other. Our Stavisht wheelers and dealers would walk around among the wagons looking for opportunities to earn some money.

The various sounds of the fair, the shouting and bargaining of buyers and sellers, the cries of drunkards and the music of the beggers playing their banduras, the crying of babies, the neighing of horses, the barking of dogs and the lowing of cattle all blended into a noisy symphony, the fair in Stavisht.

This is how the Revolution arrived in Stavisht. They began by tearing off the epaulettes of the police and army officers. No more officers, all are free and equal. Then there were meetings and manifestos and everyone marched with red flags and bands. We heard speeches which promised a free and better Russia for everyone, also for us Jews. Groups of militiamen appeared and everyone was addressed by the title "tovarishtsh" [comrade]. Night and day there were discussions about politics. Newspapers came from Kiev with screaming headlines about important events in Moscow and Petrograd.

The soldiers returned from the front with weapons. Often a soldier would get his merchandise without paying because he had a gun in his hand.

The peasants sensed that the time had come to settle accounts with the wealthy. This meant the nobles and the Jews. One fine day, it seems to me it was a market day, they attacked the Count's estate, robbed and pillaged and burned everything down. I can still see the burning buildings before my eyes. They also robbed and pillaged the distillery. They carried the liquor out by the bucketsful. The peasants had barrels of liquor available for drinking

Rumors spread of pogromchiks [pogrom participants] coming from the nearby villages and towns. Jewish travelers were attacked on their journeys, robbed and murdered. Some of the dead were brought to Stavisht to be buried. A cloud of fear hung over Stavisht and we did not know what the morrow would bring.

In the early morning of the second day of Shavuot a band of pogromchiks came into Stavisht. Their leader was Zsheleznyak. We heard gunfire on the Tarashcha road and then in town. We heard steps running up our porch and then banging on the door of our shop. No sooner had we opened the door when four bandits burst into the house, grabbed my brother Isak with revolvers in their hands, and told him to stand against the wall to be shot. They thought he was a Bolshevik. My parents and we children began to cry and beg them to let him live. My mother fell to the ground at their feet. My father put money in their hands, and finally, for a sum of money, they let him live. As soon as they left we hid him in someone's attic. Their leader, Voytsekhovski, stayed in our house the whole time the pogromchiks were in Stavisht. The "Zsheleznyaks" who occupied Stavisht killed more than twenty Jews. Among the dead were the woman dentist, Itsi Shadkhen, Hershl the cobbler's elderly mother, and others whose named I do not remember. They demanded a heavy tribute from Stavisht, of money and provisions, or they would kill all the Jews in town. Rabbi Pitsie Avraham Gaisinski, my father, and, I think, Binyamin Faynzilberg, called a meeting in the Bet Hamidrash and collected the money and provisions and saved the town from a greater catastrophe. Most of the Jews of Stavisht hid in attics and cellars. Others fled and hid out in the homes of friendly gentiles in the villages. Then the Bolsheviks came and we were able to breathe freely for a while. We were revived, but we did not feel secure. We did not know what the next day would bring.

During this time, various bands of pogromchiks passed through Stavisht and there were numerous Jewish victims. After Zsheleznyak's gang came the followers of Selyane, Makhnovtse, Zeleny, Petliura, and Denikin. When the Bolsheviks were in charge there was a bit of order and we could at least feel sure of our lives.

We heard news of the destruction wreaked by the pogromchiks in the surrounding towns. Tetiyev was completely burned to the ground and all its Jews were killed. Most of the Jews of Sokolovka were killed. We were afraid that there would be nowhere to flee. One night a small band of horsemen rode into town, arrayed themselves with guns in hand across the highway opposite the Bet Hamidrash, and demanded a large sum of money or they would kill the entire population. Once more the householders were called to a meeting and once more they redeemed their lives for money. I can still see in my mind's eye how a pogromchik led the rabbi and my father from door to door to raise the funds to save the town from slaughter.

We were in constant fear for our lives. We could not sleep through the nights. Whenever we heard a shot we would lock our gates and doors and run to hide wherever we could find a hiding place, in attics or cellars or with friendly gentiles, or in the fields and woods. Our family hid at the home of the teacher Shtsherbina whose house and school were near the church. During very bad times we hid in his garden.

When we heard rumors that the pogromchiks who had destroyed Tetiyev were headed our way, many Jews left town. Whenever a shot was heard from the distance, parents would grab their children and run towards Belaya Tserkov. They ran for their lives, taking along whatever they could carry. I did not realize that this would be the last time I would see Stavisht.

We managed to reach the village Astramagele, where a Russian teacher Mayestrenka, an acquaintance of ours, lived. We spent the night there full of fear, because we were still too close to Stavisht. Jews were not sure of surviving in peasant villages in those days. The next morning Mayestrenka took us to Belaya Tserkov with his horse and wagon. There, in the big town, the Bolsheviks were in charge. We heard that Stavisht had been set afire.

There was no pillaging or murder in Belaya Tserkov. We breathed a bit more freely. We spent the night under a roof and without hearing shots fired. We hoped for better days in the future.

[Page 119/120]

The Last Three Years in Stavisht

by Isak Golub
New York, New York

My father, Solomon Golub, had a book store with a section for musical instruments, such as violins, balalaikas, guitars, harmonicas, and gramophones and records. Our home was in the same building. Since the gramophones and records required a lot of space an entire room of our dwelling was devoted to them. We had two clerks in the shop and a maid for the house.

I was the oldest of the children. At the time of which I write I was due to graduate from the Stavisht four grade school. The two younger children attended other schools.

It was 1916 and the First World War was on. There were battles on all fronts and the Russian army suffered one defeat after another. It was in constant retreat. The Germans had already occupied Poland and the Baltic provinces.

Since we had the only shop in town that sold newspapers, many people, especially the local intelligentsia, would gather there on the porch and discuss various topics – literature, music, and the war. I remember how Luzi the teacher, Beni Mashanyanski and Beni Zunkov devised war strategy superior to what the Russian generals were doing on the front, on our porch. They used to say that Foni [derogatory name for Russia] is in bad trouble and heading for disaster. They would figure out every step and how long it would take before the Germans would occupy Stavisht.

Soon it was February 1917. There were rumblings in town. We were afraid to open our mouths. The police station was in disorder. The next day we found out that Czar Nicholas had been deposed and his brother, Michael, had taken his place. Shortly thereafter we learned that he too had been deposed and that the Duma deputy Kerensky had taken power and the Revolution had begun.

One can imagine what was going on in Russia at that time as well as in our town of Stavisht. The Jews were immediately granted full political equality.

I graduated from our school and I began to participate in the Revolution: marching with flags, singing the Marseillaise [referring to the "Worker's Marseillaise," a Russian revoluntionary anthem]. We organized ourselves into Socialist clubs. Together with Pearl Rubin we organized a club called Hoveve Tsiyon [Lovers of Zion] in Yankl the wheelwright's home. We used to meet to read about the Land of Israel, the Balfour Declaration, and the French Revolution. (Pearl Rubin is married to Yisrolik Rubin from Ksindzifke near Stavisht. They now live in White Plains, New York.)

At the end of August that same year, I left for Tarashcha to attend the Real School [Science curriculum] there. There were others there from Stavisht – Yisrael Alper, we used to call him Yisrael Heyzi, Reuven Fishlin, David Fishlin's son, and Aharon Banderov. (I have heard that Reuven Fishlin's sisters now live in Tel Aviv. I remember them as pretty young girls in Stavisht. Aharon Banderov is a doctor in Russia.) Mutsye Yaakov Yosef, the Rabbi's son, and Shelomo Rubtshanski studied in the gymnasium. (I have heard that Mutsye now lives in Jerusalem and that Shlomo Rubtshanski, now Rubin, is in America.)

In October the Bolsheviks under Lenin took over. They ceased participating in the war and demobilized the army. I remember the soldiers returning to town bringing with them what they could take away – horses and wagons, guns, machine guns, and cannons.

In a few months, a Ukrainian government was organized in Kiev headed by Vinishinski. It declared its independence from Russia. There began a power struggle. There were battles between the Bolsheviks and Ukrainians. In a short time the Bolsheviks drove the Ukrainian army out of Kiev and out of Ukraine.

This did not last long. With the aid of the German army the Ukrainian leaders re-occupied Ukraine and set up a new Ukrainian regime in Kiev. The Germans also occupied Stavisht. Everything went along at a normal pace and Jewish business prospered.

After the revolution in Germany, German power in Ukraine crumbled. The Bolsheviks took over again and life for us Jews became very dark and dismal.

Anti-Bolshevik Ukrainian bands were formed. Their liberation movement was aimed against Jews for they identified all Jews as "Bolsheviks." After every defeat by the Bolsheviks, they avenged themselves on the Jews by pillage and murder.

While I was a student in Tarashcha, Passover 1918, we heard that a partisan group was approaching to take over Tarashcha, so I returned to Stavisht. I remained there until we left the town for good. The retreating Bolsheviks from Tarashcha, with many Jews in their ranks, occupied Stavisht for a number of weeks. After they left, we Jews remained without protection.

Very early in the morning on the second day of Shavuot we heard shooting and before we knew what was happening, the town was taken over by the band which had left Tarashcha. A few thousand pogromchiks entered Stavisht. At their head were two leaders, Zsheliznak and Voytsekhovski. Two Jews were murdered upon their entrance to town – David from the Tshekhrayke [wool cleaning establishment] and Ben Tsiyon Batya Leah.

Several armed bandits entered our house. They put me up against the wall, ready to shoot, accusing me of being a Communist. My grandmother Beyla and my parents fell at their feet, kissed their hands, and begged them to wait until they had verified that I was indeed a Communist. I was at that time sixteen years old and I knew about Communism as much as Arke of Stavisht knew about rabbinics. My father offered them as much money as they wished. As soon as they heard the word money, their hearts softened and they agreed to wait until an investigation was completed. My dear mother turned gray that day.

Later I learned that Mutsye Yaakov Yosef, the Rabbi's son, had been arrested and had also been accused of Communism, and that they were looking for Reuven Fishlin as well. He was hiding out at the home of the Pshinke priest, Leyavitsh, whose children were friends of Reuven's. After a day of suffering, Mutsye was rescued from certain death.

That same day the Jews were driven into the Bet Hamidrash. I remember that when my father and I arrived there was no longer room to stand. The pogromchiks surrounded the building with guns in their hands and demanded a very large sum as ransom along with leather wear, food, and the delivery into their hands of all Jewish Communists. There were no Jewish Communists in Stavisht. The local gentiles accused the son-in-law of Hayim Meir the water-carrier of being a Communist and he paid with his life.

Our beloved Rabbi Pitsie Avraham, along with a committee of the most prominent men in town – my father Shelomo Golub, Binyamin Faynzilberg, Reuven Yagovski, Shalom Tripolski, Ya'akov Smushkin, and others whose names I do not remember – were responsible for collecting the ransom. I spent the day in the Bet Hamidrash with my father. We knew if the required ransom was not collected every Jew in town would be slaughtered.

As it happened, when the same band came to Sokolovka they murdered all of the young people in town because the ransom was not forthcoming as quickly as they demanded.

The Stavisht committee gave them everything they wanted and that is how our town was saved. The bandits stayed in our town for a week. Then the Bolsheviks began to surround us and the bandits had to retreat. As they were departing they killed 20 people. A battle began on the other side of town and the bandits started returning. As we saw them returning everyone, old and young, began to run away from Stavisht. We left everything behind, just ran for our lives. It was a fearful sight – thousands of Jews running down the roads. My parents, my grandmother, Hayale Berozi, and we children ran down the road to Belaya Tserkov. Others ran towards Voladarke. After ten days in Belaya Tserkov, we returned to Stavisht. There were only a few people in town. Little by little more people returned.

That is how the Ukrainian pogroms began. Bands of pogromchiks were formed with a few score members, with hundreds of members, and more. They struck fear into the hearts of the Jewish residents of the small towns. These bands had all kinds of names. They claimed that their goal was to free Ukraine from the Bolsheviks. Obviously, this was just lip service. Actually they robbed, destroyed, and killed whomever they pleased.

I remember when an armed bandit dressed in a Petliura uniform rode into town on his horse and demanded thirty thousand rubles threatening to kill everyone if he did not receive the money. He said that his band was waiting outside of town. He sat on his horse, gun in hand, and looked at the Bet Hamidrash waiting for what he had demanded to be given to him. Naturally he received the money. He left town. The next day we learned that he had no band and that he had, on his own, fooled us into complying with his demands. The Jews were so fearful that they gave up everything they owned to save their lives. Thus one bandit was able to fool an entire town.

The years 1917 and 1918 were full of such experiences. One band left and another entered. They pillaged and murdered. Those who escaped with their lives were lucky. Stavisht was impoverished and there were many victims.

I remember one summer evening when there was a commotion in town. There was a rumor that a Bolshevik group led by Karanivski was near. The young people in town wanted to oppose the group consisting of about ten soldiers. The young people argued that since the town owned some guns it would be possible for them to defend it.

Many people assembled in the streets. I stood next to my dear father. They consulted with each other about what to do. Suddenly we heard wild cries and shooting. We saw the bands riding their horses into town. Everyone began to run. My father and I did not have a chance to return home so we ran into an abandoned burned down house. We lay quietly on the ground so that we would not be noticed. We saw the bandits ride past several times, but they did not see us. We heard screams and shooting all night long. The next day we found out that the band had robbed, beaten, and killed twelve people. That night they killed the only dentist [female] in town. After the dreadful slaughter, a night watch of young people was organized. They were called "Habkhad."

I remember the names of some of the young people in the night watch – Luzer Golditsh, Leyb Smushkin, Bentshek Golditsh, Yosef Glants, Yehiel Snizshetski, (these now live in Boston), David Zaslavski, Moshe Monis Maryanavski, Yisrael Rubin (now in New York). There were others whose names I sadly do not remember.

As time went by there were other incidents. The Bolshevik army retreated from Crimea and came through our town. They did not harm anyone. When the Denikin group retreated from Ukraine on their way to Odessa, thousands of them rode through Stavisht, but they did not harm anyone.

From these examples it is clear that we small town Jews were ravaged by bands of Ukrainians who had always been anti-Semites and had always hated us. The Russians regarded us differently. If there are any Jews left alive after the dreadful pogroms in Ukraine it is thanks to Russia, which saved them.

I remember when Tiutiunik came through town with a band of a few thousand men. We gave them everything we had. My father and the committee worked day and night, until they collected what the band had demanded. On their way out of Stavisht they killed a Jewish hatter, whose name I do not remember.

We were able to hold out until the local gentiles began to oppose us. Then all was lost. There was no place left to hide. We had to save ourselves by fleeing to the larger cities where there was some form of government.

Not far from our town the local gentiles surrounded the town of Tetiev. They killed all of the Jews and burned down the town. The towns of Pyater [Pyatigory] and Zhashkov were also destroyed. There was nothing left for us to do but to flee. We headed for Odessa. A few weeks later Stavisht was burned down and many Jews were murdered. I met many refugees from Stavisht who had managed to escape to Odessa. We suffered quite a lot in Odessa until we were able to leave Russia. After months of wandering from one town to another we arrived in Kishinev, which was then part of Romania. We spent two years there until we had an opportunity to come to America. We arrived in New York in December 1922.

My dear mother, Beyle Golub, lived until August 1951. My dear father also lived a long life and died in February 1960. And I and my two younger brothers, Yani and Suni, and our families live in New York.

[Page 129/130]

No Longer a Melamed...

by Aharon Shohet (Arthur Shechter)
Grand Rapids, Michigan

In 1906 I was thirteen years old. I tried to study on my own, but even then I dreamed of coming to America. I could not realize my dream at that time. So I looked for a way to make a living so that I would not be idle. We were tenants at that time of Todros the maker of felt hats. His son, Itsie, married Feyge, daughter of Yisrael from the hamlet. All the neighbors were invited to the engagement party in the hamlet. We were in the same carriage as our rabbi, called Pitsie Avraham. He started a conversation with me. "Where are you studying?" he asked. When I told him that I was no longer a student and that I was planning to go to America, but I was not doing anything meanwhile, he said, "You know, teaching someone is also very meritorious." Then he looked around, for he did not, it seems, want anyone to overhear our conversation, and continued, "You know, the bride whose engagement party we are attending does not know how to read her prayers, and she has a younger sister who also does not know how to pray, so if your father and their father agree, you can remain here as their teacher, you'll get paid and you will also have a mitzva [merit]."

I thought it was a golden opportunity. Firstly, I would earn money, become an independent person. Secondly, I would be in a village surrounded by nature, which I still love to this day. I asked the rabbi to arrange the matter as soon as we arrived.

It was decided. I remained in the hamlet. On the night of the engagement party I was in seventh heaven. The next day I got a good look at my students who were both bigger and stronger than me and I became a bit worried. The first day of studies they did not even want to look at me. On the next day Yisrael persuaded the bride to come to the table and take a look at the "rebbe." On the third day the bride's sister, Nekhe, dragged her away from the study table to play with the gentile girls outside. They made jokes in Ukrainian about the "Jewish rebbe." I was so embarrassed, I started crying. When Yisrael asked me why I was not teaching his daughters, I told him that they were making fun of me and did not want to study.

He told me that I would not be able to manage them with gentleness. A teacher has to be strict, he said, and if necessary, even strike his students. Well, even the thought of striking them scared me. One was a bride and the other was a big healthy girl. But still, I felt vindicated. After all, I was in charge, and I could, if I wished, hit...

On the fourth day I demanded from my students, quite sternly, that they come in and sit down to study. The bride was a bit more polite, possibly worried that her bridegroom might find out how she was behaving and she sat down at the table. Her sister, Nekhe, did not want to come in under any circumstances. Even though she was bigger and even prettier than her sister, I went out and started to pull her into the house. It even came to blows. But you know who got hit? I, the rebbe, received a hearty slap from a big healthy girl. Very embarrassed, and perhaps fearing another slap, I walked all the way home.

That is how I ended my career as a melamed.

Itsikl

Itsikl – "Itsikl the meshugener" [crazy one] – as he was called, was really not crazy. He was mentally retarded. He was very tall and strong, with wonderful black eyes, a black beard, and he was always happy and laughing. Only one thing could anger him. He used to help Moshe the old clothes dealer carry heaps of clothing out to the market. For this his recompense was a meal. The most important thing, however, was that he was trusted to do this "delicate" job. When the idlers wanted to upset him, they would say, "You know, Itsikl, Moshe is planning to hire another 'meshugener' to replace you." Itsikl would become enraged, and with tears in his eyes he would yell and curse and declare that he would allow no other "meshugener" to take his place.

Itsikl seemed to know intuitively whenever there was a joyous occasion in town, a wedding or circumcision or engagement party, or even just a regular Kiddush [party with refreshments and wine to celebrate a holiday, Sabbath, or important occasion]. He would instantly show up among the guests, laughing his wild laugh, drinking "le-hayim" [toast, 'to life'] with the others, making "crazy" remarks, and sometimes even clever ones, which were then repeated all over town and greeted with laughter.

I remember when the richest man in town married off one of his children. Naturally Itsikl was present. The host, Motl Zaslavski, called him over and gave him a glass of brandy and said, "Drink a 'le-hayim' with me." Itsikl took his hand and said, "Le-hayim Reb Motl. What can I wish you? Wealth? You already have it. Health, you have, 'beli ayin ha-ra'ah' [without the evil eye]. Pleasure from your children, you have as well. Only one thing is left to wish you. Next year, may you have my wits, and I have yours."

Naturally, everyone appreciated the humor of this remark. No one was ever angry with Itsikl, not even the host.

However, the Germans lacked a sense of humor. During the First World War, they became angry when Itsikl did not halt as they had ordered him… [implication that he was shot].

[Page 135/136]

A Bundle of Memories

by Aharon Weissman
Tel Aviv

Aharon Weissman

I myself am not a Stavishter. My connection to the town derives from my father and my wife, may they rest in peace, who were born in Stavisht. But I remember the town because I was there as a young boy, visiting my grandfather, Shemulik Moshe-Leyzers [i.e. the son of Moshe Leyzer] and my grandmother Yehudit, may her memory be for a blessing. My grandfather, may he forgive me, was not much of a businessman. But my grandmother was a respected and clever merchant and had a fine general store which she managed with the help of her red-bearded and very pious younger son Avraham.

How did one travel in those days? With a wagon, of course. The distance between my birthplace, Uman, and Stavisht was 70 viorst, and it was a full day and night journey, with a stopover for the night at Sokolifke or Kanele.

I remember those journeys to this day. I especially remember the coachman. One was nicknamed "Barukh She-amar" ["Blessed is He who said" – beginning of a prayer] and the other was nicknamed "Olam Ha-ba" [the world to come, the afterlife]. These names were derived linguistically thus: The first one's given name was Barukh, so the Stavishter jokesters added the word "she-amar" from the prayer book. The name of the second coachman was Aba, actually Avraham – Aba, so they prefaced it with the word "olam." [Translator's note: The "h" is not pronounced in Ukrainian Yiddish, so it would be pronounced Oylem aba.]

Once, when I was still a young boy, I saw the Stavisht wagon coming to Uman. I immediately ran out and shouted, "Reb Barukh She-amar, did you bring me a letter from my grandfather?" (The coachmen also served as letter-carriers in those days.)

"Who are you, little boy?"

"I am the son of Hayim-Shemuelik-Moshe-Leyzers" [i.e. Hayim the son of Shemuelik the son of Moshe Leyzer].

"Not this time, little boy, perhaps another time."

I had the "honor" of going to Stavisht and back with Olam Ha-ba. The passage of time has dimmed my memory of how he looked, but I still remember his team of horses and the wagon. It was a big Ukrainian covered wagon which had been Judaized and had been refurbished "to the nth degree" [said sarcastically]. The front section was padded with a bit of rag-covered straw. The important passengers sat under the cover made of old patched sacks. Opposite them, like hens in a cage, sat the less important passengers, women, and girls. The ordinary passengers sat on the sides with their feet on stirrups made of boards tied on with ropes. New passengers kept coming aboard and outside the town a few more people got on. Nevermind, it did not reach scandalous proportions. Anyway, everyone was all shook up from the trip and the passengers started to catch their breaths and straighten out a bit only after we were out in the fresh air. As long as it was dry outdoors we managed somehow. The poor horses gasped and quivered and shook their heads nervously.

On all sides of the wagon were hung packages, boxes, bundles, and baskets of all sizes. From Uman to Stavisht they were full of merchandise and on the trip back to Uman they were full of the local products – goose fat and cracklings. Stavisht exported these products to Uman and other cities, even as far as Odessa.

I remember the boulevard in Stavisht – a long passageway in front of the Count's estate. Stavisht belonged to Count Branicki and the nobles who managed the estate lived there. The young people would promenade on the boulevard and the older folk would walk there to "get a breath of fresh air."

Stavisht was also distinguished by the Zionist Kloyz. The elite of the householders, the more enlightened ones, refined young sons-in-law and "intelligentsia" built their own synagogue. This was a great innovation in those days because most Jews were opponents of Zionism.

I especially remember the teacher from Stavisht who taught in Uman. I studied two semesters with him, Pentateuch and Rashi [commentary on the Bible]. He had a very hoarse voice and bulging eyes. He was very good-natured. He never hit his students. It seems that he did not even own a whip. When my father, peace upon him, would come back from a visit to Stavisht, my teacher, Shimon-Ber, would come to greet him and his first question was always, "Who has died in Stavisht?"

This is my little bundle of memories of Stavisht, a fine little town with dear inhabitants.

[Page 139/140]

To My Little Town Stavisht

by Batya Orland
Tel Aviv, Israel

With sap-filled green branches on the trees in the forest
Sandy roads like fine gold
White little houses with straw roofs
My little town stands lonely, at world's end.

In the early evenings the winds would blow
A herd of goats would chew the grass
The earth sown with grain
The meadows, the bushes, clothed in green.

The carefree gentiles stroll in the streets
Somewhere, a fearful boy and girl are driven as by jest
The humble congregation streams out of the synagogue
And the old miller shuts down the mill.

My lonely little town, my home and my cradle
My happy youth, this is your victory
I remember your frightening winters
But clinging together, joy without end.

You are my youth, you are my song
I am never weary of recalling you
Your sweet secrets accompany me
Are with me every year, every hour, every day.

You have been destroyed, my little town
You stand forlorn, mourning forever
We are both weary and worn out
I here at home and you far away.

[Page 141/142]

What I Remember

by Naftali Rubin (Rubtshanski)

I was too young to remember any incidents about myself. However, I remember the stories told by my parents, Binyamin and Sara, and my relatives.

There were stories about serving in the army:

Only one of my Uncle Shike's five sons served the Czar – Nahum. The others managed, thank God, to get out of serving. I remember the story about Fayvl hiding under Aunt Mize's quilt and she lay on top of him so that he would not be seen. I still cannot understand how the policeman could not see him, he was so long.

Why didn't Jews want to serve? Jews considered themselves the Chosen People. In the army they became third or even fourth class citizens. What did they need this for?

I remember a ritual question about a slaughtered cow. In such a situation people ran to the rabbis. They researched all the sources all night long. Then they called my father and asked him how much of a loss he would endure if the cow was deemed non-kosher. My father replied, A lot of money! (I do not remember how much). They looked in the sources again and decided: Forty pounds [of meat] should be given to the poor and the rest could be sold.

I heard many stories about the pogroms, how they shot and robbed and murdered the Jews, how they shot 42 young boys and set the beards of old men on fire. How a bandit put a revolver into my mother's mouth and from that time she hiccupped all her life. How my father was locked into a cellar without food or water for three days. How my grandfather was murdered.

Once, all the Jews hid in a cellar, and my sister Rose, who was then about four months old, began to cry. They wanted to strangle her, so that her cries would not be heard, but my mother began to nurse her so she stopped crying.

Before we could come to America, we first had to escape from Russia. We had to cross the Dnieper River to Romania. We hid in a gentile home until we could rent a boat. Very often the gentiles would swindle or murder the Jews.

My sisters Hayke and Dani were always afraid to go sailing on the ocean because they saw their girlfriend drown when her boat overturned.

[Page 143/144]

Scenes of Childhood

by David Kohen (son of Avraham Sokanik)

Sabbath in Stavisht

The town of my birth was called Stavisht. It was quite small, but very beautiful, with two large rivers on both sides of the town. It looked like an island surrounded by water.

One river was called "Sandy" and the other "Gedalkes" [According to a number of atlases consulted, there was one river, "Gniloi Tikich," "Hnylyi Tikych" in Ukrainian. "Gedalke" may be a nickname for the Russian version of the name. The atlas does not name a second river. A detailed photograph of the town shows large ponds coming off the river. One of these may be the "Sandy" river here mentioned.] The Sandy River was very clean. When one bathed there one could see one's reflection as if in a mirror. The men bathed on one shore and the women on the other. There were many kinds of fish in the rivers: carp, tench, and others. The fish were very tasty. People who used to come there from big cities would say that they had never eaten such good fish and they would never forget the taste.

The entrance to town was very beautiful. On one side were the houses of the nobility with trees and fragrant flowers, too beautiful for words. On the other side of town was a large forest with many trees. There was good air to breathe from the rivers, air such as one finds in resorts. It made people feel healthy and young.

It was a Jewish town with 600 families, five prayer houses and a big synagogue. All the artisans prayed in the big synagogue: tailors, cobblers, hatters, blacksmiths, carpenters. The Sokolifker Hasidim prayed in the Sokolifker Kloyz. There were also a Talner Kloyz, a Mekarever Kloyz, and a Bet Hamidrash. Every holy place had its own rabbi and his followers.

No Christians lived in town. There were two villages nearby. One was called Raskashne, with 10,000 Christians, and the other was called Pshinke with 5000 Christians. Of course I never counted the population. I am only reporting what people said.

Most people were poor but lived quiet and contented lives. Some earned a living as artisans and some as merchants. It was a town with many shops selling textiles, groceries, sewing notions, hardware. Merchants made a good living. Some sold shoddy clothing on the street, others sold coops, kerchiefs, pins, soap. The small shopkeepers would sit next to their shops waiting for customers to pass by, then they would pull the customers, the peasants, into their little shops.

One day a week there was a fair. Many peasants would come to town from the surrounding villages bringing their produce to sell. They would earn much money, then they would purchase everything they needed from the Jews. Everyone earned a few rubles for the Sabbath from the fair.

Most Jews worked very hard to make a living. Rich people had bigger and nicer houses and poor people had small ones. But when the holy Sabbath came, every Jew enjoyed a spiritual pleasure. Every housewife baked halla for the Sabbath and prepared good fish and poultry.

The Sabbath foods filled the streets with their fragrance. A fresh layer of yellow clay had been spread over the floor of the poorer homes. There was a clean tablecloth on the table and two beautiful loaves were covered with a clean cloth. A holy atmosphere reigned in every home during the Sabbath.

As the husband came home from the synagogue, he was greeted by his wife and children. He said, "Gut Shabbos," said "Shalom aleikhem" [prayer said upon returning home from the synagogue on Friday night] and made Kiddush. His wife brought the fish and the other good foods to the table. Then the Jew was free of care, did not think about making a living. He was quiet and content. When people met each other in the street one would say, "Gut Shabbos" and the other would respond, "Gut yor" [good year]. People greeted each other with sincerity. Sometimes a quarrel would break out in the synagogue over the order of the aliyot [the order in which one was called to the Torah], but after the prayers were over they would make peace with each other.

A Wedding Ceremony

When the parents of a bride celebrated their daughter's engagement and wrote tenaim [engagement contract], they would deposit the dowry with a trustee. The bridegroom did not want the money to remain with the bride's father. The bride's family was responsible for making the wedding.

Two weeks before the wedding, tailors were hired to go to the bride's home to sew the clothing for the wedding. Every day was like a holiday. Friends and neighbors would come to visit and they would drink a "le hayim."

The bride and the groom had to fast on their wedding day. Before the ceremony the groom would go to the bride and cover her face with her veil. The ceremony was performed [outdoors] near the synagogue.

After the ceremony the couple would return to the bride's home to eat something. Men and women would not sit together. The fish course would be served.

After the fish, two large plates and a tray would be set on the table and one of the bride's relatives would start to call out which gifts were being presented by the bride's family. People would give money, 50 kopeks, a ruble, etc. These gifts would go to the bride's father. Afterwards the groom's relatives would present gifts, which would go to the young couple.

After the ceremony and after the festive meal, the band played and the guests danced all night long. Then the band would escort the relatives home playing all the while. After the wedding there were seven days of "sheva berakhot" [benedictions said at festival meals for the seven days after a wedding].

My Childhood Years

There were five children in our family, three sons and two daughters. My parents were considered well-to-do.

When I was three years old I was sent to study with a melamed. His name was Yosef Ginendel's, after his mother. He had a bahelfer [teacher's assistant] to help with the children. There were about 20 boys. I did not want to go to heder. My mother went to the teacher to ask for advice. The teacher sent her to the bahelfer. The bahelfer said he would come to take me every day and he would bring me home in the evenings, but he wanted to be paid. He wanted to eat in our home two days a week and he wanted 25 kopeks every month. My mother agreed. Every day he came to take me to heder, but I did not go willingly and it was hard work for the bahelfer.

My parents tried to find a way to make me go to heder willingly. How would I learn to love school and study? My mother undertook the task to make me love school. I loved my mother dearly and I used to love to listen to the stories she told.

Once on a Sabbath my mother called me to her and said, "My child, I want to tell you a story about something that actually happened to you. Listen carefully to every word I say." She told me that when I was a year-and-a-half old I was very sick. The doctors could not help me. There was a big doctor in town named Horekh. He was called to examine me. His answer was that he could do nothing for me. I had a boil in my throat and it was in a spot he could not reach.

"My child," she said, "when we saw how bad it was and that the doctors could not do anything for you, we took you to a rabbi. When we came there we began to cry and told him that the doctors said they could not help you, and we pleaded with the rabbi for a remedy.

"The rabbi replied, 'Go home and God will help him. Even a bit of snuff can help. Doctors do not know everything. God is a doctor and He can help.'"

"We came back home and when we arrived you were 90 percent dead. We cried and wept. Then a poor man came in for a donation. He asked, 'What happened here? Why is everyone weeping and crying?' He was told that there was a sick child who was almost dead. He asked, 'Where is this sick child?'" He was taken into the room where I lay. The poor man came over to me and looked at me. He took out his snuff box. My mother happened to raise her hand and accidentally knocked the snuff box out of his hand. The snuff fell all over my face. I started sneezing and the boil opened. The doctor was called and he said it was a miracle. He had not believed that I would recover.

My mother finished telling the story and she said to me, "My child, do you know why the rabbi helped you? When he was a little boy he loved to go to heder and he loved to study and he knows how to study. God loves everyone who studies and God listens to him and helps whoever asks Him for help. So my child, if you will love to go to heder and learn, God will love you and you will also be able to help sick Jews to become well."

My mother's words made a strong impression. I began to go to heder every day willingly and became the best student. I studied there until I was 8 years old.

My second teacher was Leyzer Bogaslavski. The richer children went to him. There I stayed until I was twelve years old. Then I was sent to study with Barukh Ben Tsiyon. He was the best teacher in town. The richest children, even big youths, studied there. I was the youngest. They did not want to be my friends. The teacher asked his son Yisrolik to be my friend and study partner, and he was. However, he did not do this of his free will.

Before Purim the teacher told us that he was planning a festive meal and every student should bring 15 kopeks two days before Purim. Everyone brought in the money except for two students who were absent. The teacher did not know why they had not come. Since they lived not far from me, he asked me to go to see them and see why they had not some to heder. When I asked them why they had not come, they began to cry that their mother did not want to give them any money and that is why they could not come. I told my mother the story about these students. They did not have a father. Their mother did not want to give them the 30 kopeks, so they could not come to the festive Purim meal. My mother heard the story and asked me, "My child, is it right that they should not be together with you because they cannot pay 30 kopeks?" I answered, "It is not right!" She continued, "What should we do so that they can come?" My mother used to give me ten kopeks every week, so I said to her, "Give me 30 kopeks and I will give the money to them and for three weeks you will not give me any money."

My mother kissed me for my reply. She gave me the 30 kopeks and told me, "You should always behave like this, help everyone."

I immediately brought the 30 kopeks to the two boys and they became very happy and returned to heder. My mother told me not to tell anyone what I had done. From that time on these boys were my best friends in heder so that my childhood years were not bad.

I have lived through good times and very bad times. I have experienced pogroms and there were times I could not spend the night in the same place I had spent the day. We ran from one town to another and it was bad everywhere. I have lived on foreign soil and even in peace time Jews could not live how they wanted to. They were made to feel foreign. I want to recall an episode.

There was a gentile who worked for us. He was very loyal to us. In the time of unrest we hid in his home. Once, while I was hiding in his house, some neighbors came to see him. I heard them talk about the Jews and how they should be wiped out and robbed because they have sucked the blood from the Christians. My friend responded, "They should be killed." When his neighbors left, we came out of hiding. I told him I had heard.

He answered that he loved my family, but that he hated all Jews. I did not go back to his house.

[Page 153/154]

A Story of Evil Spirits

by Gedalyahu Tserkas

My father, the late Hayim Yekl Tserkas, was a progressive person relatively speaking for that time and place. He wanted his sons to study Hebrew and not be ignorant of the Talmud. He worked hard for the founding of a fine modern school in Stavisht. It was called a "Heder Metukan" [proper school] in those days. The subjects taught there were Bible, History, Grammar and also Talmud for beginners. I studied these subjects with a private teacher, Mr. Yisrael Shumski.

It was not easy to carry out the plan to start the school. Many people were opposed to the idea. The house which was to become the modern school had a large brick oven as was common in those days. When the oven was dismantled the local melamdim [plural of melamed, teachers of young children] started a rumor that the house was haunted by evil spirits. In order to frighten the parents who had planned to enroll their children in school, they said that hen tracks had been found in the ashes of the stove. (As is known, evil spirits have chicken feet).

Once, when the sexton, old Moshe Neta, came in to clean up the house, he received a terrible blow on his head from a lectern which had been balanced over the door. The frightened sexton was convinced that this was a trick of the evil spirits and ran out and told everyone what had happened to him. There were people who claimed to have witnessed evil spirits in that house.

But my father did not give up his plan. He kept assuring everyone that these were lies, and in order to prove his point he said he would spend a night in the house with the door locked from the outside. My father went in and many people participated in locking the door and windows from the outside. They were sure that they would find my father dead the following morning and then they would have a sumptuous funeral, but he awoke hale and hardy. Instead a festive meal was held to celebrate the victory over the evil spirits.

[Page 155/156]

Days of Pogroms

by Yisrael Senderovitsh
(son of Pinhas Hayim Leyb Senderovski)
Toronto, Ontario, Canada

As long as I live I shall not forget the day that Zelezniak's band came into town. On that day my family had its first victim, my dear brother-in-law, my sister's husband, Yitshak "the Kohen Gadol" [High Priest] as he was known.

This is how it happened. Shimele the tailor lived next door to us. A bandit came in and found their daughter Brakha. He was drunk. He began to chase her and she ran out the back door and ran into our house. She ran out of the other door and the bandit chased her. When he did not find her, he saw my dear brother-in-law sleeping in his bed. He took his rifle and shot him. Then he lay down in the other bed. My sister and my mother started screaming. Two bandits came in and removed the drunken bandit.

Four people were killed that day. We men stayed in the Bet Hamidrash all day long. It took a long time until we collected the money Zelezniak demanded. We finally achieved it. I was the last one to leave. He knew about the dead and begged our forgiveness. He said that his followers were very wild, he could not restrain them. He asked which families had suffered victims. As I was one of these, Zelezniak gave me 6000 rubles for my sister.

This is how we began to live in fear of losing our lives. We did not spend the night in the place we spent the day. The bands would come in one after another.

Now I shall tell what happened to me personally:

Malkah Tsiadiak and her children, three girls and a boy, lived with us. One of her daughters, Libe, became my bride. She died too young and I still mourn for her. She was a seamstress and had many friends in town. Whenever a band showed up, her Christian friends would come   to take her and her family to hide them until it was quiet again.

The night of horrors! When Denikin and his band came into town, one of Libe's friends took us all to her house for a few days. Another friend invited us for Friday night and said she would make a party for us. We could not refuse the invitation because we were their guests. We agreed to come. Friday night, my wife and her sister Hayke and her brother Hershl Sivak and I went to the party.

We found about ten young men and women who received us very nicely. We had a good time. The house was not far from the highway. Suddenly the door opened and four bandits of Denikin's band burst in. We Jews became very frightened. The bandits stopped the dancing and asked what was going on. When they were told it was a party, they started to leave. Then they turned back and told me and Hershl Sivak to go with them. At first we thought they were kidding around because they had acted so friendly at first, but then they started talking more harshly to us. My wife and her sister started to cry and beg that they not hurt us. Nothing helped. The bandits wanted us to go with them. The Christian young men did not say a word. Two of the Christian girls came over to Libe and said, "Don't cry Libke, we won't let them take them." Then the Christian youths ran over and said, "Enough. Tell us what you want, or leave this house at once. If not, you will not get out alive." The bandits said to us, "We do not want to see you here. We did not want to frighten you. Leave at once because other members of the band will come and will shoot you. It is terrible in town." They left the house.

Right after they left we returned to the place we had been before. But we were afraid to stay there, so we crept up into an attic and spent the whole night there. Early in the morning we came down from the attic, shivering and shaking.

This is how we spent our youth.

When we heard the news from Kaminke, I said goodbye to my parents and left. I never saw my father again. Five years after I left he died of sorrow.

[Page 159/160]

Yitshak Shadkhen
[The name Shadkhen means matchmaker]

A Memorial for a Gentle Soul

by Berl Rubin (Divinski)
Philadelphia, Pennsylvania

Itsi Shadkhen was the only son of Hersh-Mendl Shadkhen, who also had four daughters. At that time we rented a dwelling behind his house. One hot summer day there was a rumor that a band was coming into Stavisht. That night we saw the officers of the band in the house across the way, playing cards. Hersh-Mendl, never fainthearted, smiled and went out of the house. He invited them to play cards in his house along with him. We believed that nothing would happen to us.

In the morning two bandits came in. They searched every nook and cranny in my house and in Hersh-Mendl's. He was not at home at the time. The girls jumped out of the window and ran away. The only ones left were Itsi, his mother Haya, and my wife and I. Itsi and Haya escorted the bandits to the door, then one of the bandits took his gun and shot Itsi. The bullet went through his right leg and into his mother's abdomen. Itsi lay on the floor of the corridor. We took him into the house. Then we brought a pail of water and put cold compresses on his foot. My wife put cold compresses on Haya's abdomen but the blood kept flowing.

This lasted for about two or three hours. Then Hersh-Mendl came home and saw the disaster. He did not say a word but ran out and came back with some people who carried out his wife and son, put them in a wagon, and brought them to the hospital. The bullet was removed from Haya's abdomen and she recovered. But Itsi had lost too much blood and he was dead by the time they arrived at the hospital.

Itsik Hersh Mendl was about eighteen or nineteen years old and was taller than his father, taller than anyone in the house. He had been away from home for about two years, studying in Elizavetgrad, and had just come home for vacation. During those two years he had developed both physically and culturally.

He was very handsome. His dark eyes caressed you when he spoke to you. His debates with the other young men were amazing. He knew so much and could answer every question so logically. He listened to others calmly and responded with grace. Honor to his memory!

[Page 161/162]

A Memorial for Stavisht!

by Moshe Gulka
Toronto, Ontario, Canada

When I left Stavisht at the end of 1906 it was a traditional Jewish town, with about 1500 Jewish inhabitants, whose constitution was the Shulhan Arukh [code of laws compiled by Joseph Caro, 1488-1575] and whose judges were the rabbis, even though they were without political, social, or economic rights under the Tsarist regime. Their only source of income was petty commerce.

The peasants of the nearby villages would come to the fairs every week to sell their agricultural products and in exchange buy clothing and household utensils as well as to repair farm implements and other necessities. There was a bakery that made bagels exclusively for the market days.

There was no industry in town, so naturally there was no proletariat. Since the town was not on the railroad, connections with other towns was made via waggoners and their coaches.

It is easy to imagine how poverty lurked in most homes in town. Nevertheless the town had two rabbis: Yaakov Yosef, the rabbi of the gentry; and Pitsie Avraham (Gaisinski) the rabbi of amkha [the simple folk]; four ritual slaughterers; a Bet Midrash; a synagogue (the cold synagogue); a Makarov, a Sokolovka, a Talnoye, and a Zionist kloyz; a Bikur holim [visiting the sick]; and a Talmud Torah for poor children. The expenses were covered, more or less, by the takse [tax on ritual slaughter used for communal purposes]. Naturally there was also a slaughter house, a bathhouse, and two cemeteries under communal supervision.

And so people struggled and lived and earned from each other. In the spiritual sense they were like one poor family which helps each other out, with some exceptions.

Everyone felt he was a child of God and that God treated him according to his worth. Others felt as if they were special, if their situation was better than that of the rest.

Geographically the town was 50 viorst [about 33 miles] from Belaya Tserkov (called in Yiddish Shvarts Timeh), 30 viorst from Tarashcha, and 15 viorst from Zhashkov, from which Moshe Dayan's father comes (as I read in the Tog-Morgen Zhurnal).

By the way, I should like to mention that a member of our committee, Galant [Moshe Galant] is, I believe, my uncle Moshe Katsebivker's step-son. My father was Nahum Katsebivker.

And now I should like to make a suggestion:

I believe that the people who lived in Stavisht in previous generations believed in the transmigration to the Holy Land after death. All of the tombstones have certainly been demolished by the present Communist regime and, let us be frank, by the Ukrainian population. It would be a good idea to buy a piece of land in Erets Yisrael and to plant trees there as a memorial to Stavisht. It should cost about $1500 and so we will immortalize our ancestors' memories. A book will be forgotten as time goes by. The same committee should undertake this project.

[Page 165/166]

Personalities

by Y. Rubin
New York, New York

Shemuel Ba'al Takseh (Shmulik Avraham'tshes) was an upright man, learned and clever. He lived in his own house, near Nahman Rozenblit, the holder of special privileges from the Stavisht Town Authority. In his old age he sold the house for a Zionist synagogue and school. He dealt in lumber and wooden utensils, barrels, buckets, and so on. He knew how to read some Russian and could write addresses in English. People would come from all over town for him to write the addresses on the letters and postcards they sent to America and England.

He loved to tell stories and crack jokes and to play tricks. Shmulik often visited his neighbor, Nahman Rozenblit. Nahman had three sons and some daughters. His oldest son, Simha, left for America and came back after a few years, dressed very nicely with a fedora, considered a luxury in those days. Only the intelligentsia and well-to-do people could afford such a hat.

Obviously a pious Jew would not wear a fedora. Shmulik Avraham'tshes was a pious Jew. He prayed in the Sokolovka Kloyz where Rabbi Pitsie Avraham prayed. When Simha came from America wearing a fedora, Shmulik came to greet him. He complimented him on his nice hat. Simha said to him, "Reb Shmuel, I will give you the hat if you wear it to shul today."

Shmulik agreed to the conditions. Early Saturday morning, a beautiful day, the sun was shining, it was dry and warm when all Jews were walking to their various synagogues. Shmulik came along with a red kerchief around his neck, his talis [a fringed undergarment worn by males] visible under his coat and the fedora on his head. He was followed by a crowd which kept getting larger. He was escorted to the synagogue and back to his home. This was one of the tricks he played. Of course, he kept the fedora.

Mother of Leah Mazur
mother-in-law of Efrayim "Tetievsky"

[Translator's note. This is my mother's aunt Sima Tetievsky.
Her daughter Leah married Efrayim Mazur (their photos are
on opposite page) and I cannot figure out why the name "Tetievsky"
appears after Efrayim. I should like to suggest that we caption it Sima Tetievsky,
mother of Leah Mazur, mother-in-law of Efrayim Mazur.]

I recall another incident with Shmulik. In our town there was a man named Hayim Ya'akov Tsherkes (Hayim Ya'akov Leybushes) who sold wine. He had a wine cellar and every Passover eve Shmulik would come with an empty gallon bottle to buy wine for Passover. As was known, Shmulik was a very pious Jew and observed all the laws and customs of Moses and Israel. One Passover eve he came to Hayim Ya'akov with two bottles to buy wine.

Hayim Ya'akov knew that Shmulik's children no longer lived at home and that only he and his wife were there and wondered why he needed two bottles full. He asked him, "Reb Shmuel, how come you have two bottles? Do you have guests?"

He replied, "I should like to have the wine in one bottle and the water in the other and I shall mix them according to my taste [implying that the seller watered his wine]. Shmulik used to make such jokes quite often. He knew how to get along with old and young. He was a witty man, an important Jew. He died at the time of the First World War at 80, honor his memory.

Efrayim Mazur was a learned Jew who knew not only Yiddish and Hebrew but also knew Russian very well. He was observant but not fanatic. He used to study day and night and his wife took care of business and he helped out from time to time. People used to come and ask his advice and often appointed him mediator in business or personal conflicts. I knew him very well because we prayed in the same synagogue, the Makarov Kloyz. I was very young and I had a great deal of respect for him.

Mazur Leah
Wife of Efrayim Mazur (in America)

Efrayim Mazur
The bookkeeper of Stavisht Bank

In former years there was no bank in Stavisht. As time went by they founded a credit union where people could borrow a few hundred rubles when they needed money, for little interest, a sort of Free Loan, and Efrayim Mazur became the bookkeeper there. This bank was under the administration of the Government and the books were kept in the Russian language. Efrayim Mazur was the manager.

Some time later an official bank was founded in Stavisht. Binyamin Faynzilber of the apothecary shop became the president and Efrayim Mazur was the bookkeeper. The bank lasted until after the First World War, until the pogroms of 1918-1920. It was impossible to keep it open during the pogroms and most of the Jews left the town.

Efrayim Mazur was a person of good understanding, logical and loyal and upright, before God and people. You could trust him and you did not have to bribe him. It is hard to find such honorable and fine people nowadays.

[Page 171/172]

In Hiding

by Dobe Samet (Sheynes)
Montreal, Quebec, Canada

I do not remember what year it was, but I only remember it was New Year's Eve. My two sisters and I hid at the home of Doctor Horekh. My parents and my brothers hid at the home of the doctor's cook, Dabitski.

It was the time when the Bolsheviks were pursuing the Denikins. As they passed through Stavisht, a large group of Denikins came to stay at the home of Doctor Horekh. When they saw me they asked who I was. I was dressed like a gentile girl.

Horekh's wife answered that I was a Polish seamstress who worked for her. All the officers brought me their torn trousers to repair. My sisters and I sat above the oven free of fear. The officers saw how I patched their trousers and pricked my fingers. They were pleased with my work and some of them gave me presents.

On the second day a detachment of Bolsheviks arrived and the Denikins left. My sisters and I remained at the home at Doctor Horekh. His wife said to me, "I saved you from the Denikins, so I want you to save me from the Bolsheviks." (But what could I do for her?) She said, "After all, the Bolsheviks are a Jewish government."

The first group that came in immediately started robbing. They looked for the doctor's daughter Marusye. They raped her, broke everything in the house, took all the liquor, and ordered that food be prepared for them. (You should see the people who gave the orders!) I still remember that I cooked a big pot of borsht, who knows what it tasted like. They were so drunk they did not know what was happening.

Among the Bolsheviks there was a big, heavyset bandit. He called me over and said, "You know, I like you. I want to take you along with me." You can imagine how I felt.

After they had drunk so much, they fell asleep. Around midnight I said to my sisters, "Let's run away!" But where could we go? We ran to Pshinke [gentile village]. There was a writer of the peace court, Ardenski, who lived there. I knocked on the door. He let us in and allowed us to sleep in his attic covered with featherbeds which my parents had hidden there. In the morning he told us to leave, he was afraid to keep us there. So we went home, where we found my parents and brothers.

[Page173/174]

One Night's Experiences

by Berl Rubin (Divenski)
Philadelphia, Pennsylvania

It seems like a dream, as if it had only just happened. It was a long time after the Russian Revolution. We heard about all the dreadful pogroms and massacres of Jews. We also heard that in many towns Jews had self-defense groups that fought the bandits, in Boguslav and Tetiev.

One afternoon a son of Yisrael Tsinis came to see me. He had been in the army and had recently returned home. When I asked what I could do for him he replied that he knew that I was interested in organizing a self-defense organization in Stavisht and he wanted to join. He knew where to buy weapons at very little cost. For twenty five rubles he could bring sufficient arms. Would he also teach us how to hold the weapons and how to shoot? "Of course!" Tsinis' son cried out, his eyes staring at me and his face turning red.

We decided to keep the matter secret and that he would come to see me the following week. He came, got the money, and left for Belaya Tserkov to buy the arms. I was busy organizing the self-defense group. We had about twenty-five members, among whom I remember Leyb Sheynor and Moshe Kohen. It was decided to keep everything completely secret.

It was deceptively quiet in town, but it was a seething cauldron beneath. People spread rumors and the panic kept growing. Tsinis returned with twenty revolvers and a few rifles. More volunteers joined up. Everyone swore secrecy and to fight to the last breath.

The arms were well hidden. When we drilled everyone got his weapon and came to the center. Tsinis was the commander. I was the oldest one there. Some days passed. People got a bit calmer. We thought no one knew about the self-defense, the weapons, and so on. But it seems that the secret was out and everywhere we went we heard talk of "self-defense." Old and young, small and big talked about it, some with approval, some with disapproval, and there were rumors about who was involved.

A few days later, on a Tuesday afternoon, the door opened and Rabbi Pitsie Avarham and Hirsh Mendl Shadkhen came in and wanted to meet with me immediately. "Listen Berl," Pitsie Avraham said, "It's quiet in town, and let us hope it continues this way and we won't have any troubles. You are well organized and you have weapons and we know that the gentiles know about this. We talked with the police and they demand that we give up the weapons and we want you to do so. They promise that all will be well."

I argued with them for over an hour but it was no use. It was decided that I would talk it over with the organization and the arms would be handed over to the representatives of the congregation.

A few days later a band of about ten or eleven bandits came in and we heard shooting immediately. I let the members of the self-defense know, but what was the use? We did not have any weapons.

I and my son, ten or eleven years old, and Leyb Shneynor's went out to the marketplace near the big inn opposite Smaliar's. There were four young gentiles about sixteen to eighteen years old, leaning on rifles, standing apart from each other, so that it was possible to knock the rifles out from under them. The Jews came there to see what the situation was. Mendl Hanapolske [Ganapolski] stood nearby and called out, "No, children, I shall take them away, give them lunch, and everything will be fine."

Mendl took the four boys and then we heard terrible cries from some houses and saw horsemen coming out of the narrow streets and riding all over town. My son and I ran away. We ran past Feldsher Tadarke's house to the Gedalke River and found a little boat where we spent the night. All though the night we heard rifle fire, the sounds of breaking glass, and screams and cries. Toward dawn all became quiet and we returned home.

[Page 177/178]

Our Town Stavisht

by Yisrael Shumski (Tsinis)
Havatselet, Israel

The town of Stavisht was one of the properties of Count Branicki. His main office was at the back of town. The mansions in which his officials lived, the homes of the doctor and the midwife and the hospital buildings, formed a kind of enclave within the town. There were two churches in town, Russian Orthodox and Catholic. There was also an infirmary, two streams, upon which stood two flour mills leased by Jews, and two distilleries of wine and beer. The peasants lived on the outskirts.

There were about 10,000 Jews. Many of them were artisans while others were wheat or egg merchants, butchers, and storekeepers. The stores and butcher shops were in the center of town. In front of them was the marketplace. There were stands, most of them managed by women. They sold all kinds of merchandise: needles, threads, colored ribbons for the gentile girls, soap, etc. There were also stands for selling bread and baked goods. Women sat on the ground and sold all kinds of fruits: apples, pears, cherries, etc. The wives of the butchers sold intestines and lungs to the poor inhabitants. Gentile women also sat in the marketplace and sold pork to the peasants.

The fair was held on a Sunday, every two weeks. The peasants of the entire vicinity would bring their produce to sell and they would buy what they needed. They would bring wheat, cattle, horses, skins of cattle, foxes, rabbits and martens, etc. In the summertime they would bring fruit to sell. The peasant women would bring the heavy cloth they had woven, canvas fibers and stalks of flax, poultry and eggs. In the wintertime they would bring geese to sell. Some families would buy the geese, fatten them up, fry the fat, and send it to Odessa to be sold.

In the late afternoon, after the peasants had sold their produce, they would buy boots, boards, nails, tar and utensils. In the winter, during their fast days, they would buy salted and dried fish. The women would buy dry goods, sugar, oil, flour, etc.

This was the economic situation. And now, as to the spiritual situation: There were five synagogues in town:

1. The synagogue where the ordinary people prayed;
2. The Bet Ha-midrash for the Skvira Hasidim and others;
3. The Sokolovka Kloyz;
4. The Talnoye Kloyz;
5. The Makarov Kloyz.

At the beginning of the twentieth century a Zionist prayer house was built. There was a Talmud Torah where the sons of the more affluent Jews, mostly Zionists, studied and paid tuition fees. The Talmud Torah was supported by the organization called in Hebrew "Hevrat Mefitse Haskalah ben Hayehudim" [Society for the Promotion of Culture Among the Jews of Russia] located in St. Petersburg. There were teachers of Hebrew and Bible for beginners as well as teachers of Hebrew grammar for the older boys. Students who completed the courses at the Talmud Torah were eligible to enter the High School for beginners [Middle School] run by the government which had four grades. Many children were able to do so for secular subjects were taught at the Talmud Torah as well as Hebrew subjects. The tuition fee was very low, six rubles a year.

There was a hospital in town and the two doctors of the Count's estate also served the Jews. The Catholic drug store would supply medicine free if prescribed by these doctors (they were paid for by the Count). There were also a Jewish paramedic and two Christian paramedics and two drug stores owned by Jews that would sell medicines prescribed by the doctors or the paramedics. There was an old fashioned bathhouse. Railroad tracks were laid, but were not used for many years.

In 1897, the year of the First Zionist Congress, a Zionist organization was founded in our town and I was its secretary until 1915. At that time the Hevrat Mefitse Haskalah, mentioned previously, sent me to Kremenits in the province of Volyn to serve as a teacher. The pious people in town opposed Zionism and the others were indifferent; nevertheless, we sold more than 400 shares in the Colonial Bank headquartered in London [Jewish Colonial Trust (Bank) founded by the World Zionist Organization in 1898, based in London, to develop Jewish colonization of Palestine].

At the time of the pogroms when the murderers Denikin and Petliura were passing through, I was no longer in Stavisht. This is what I remember about my town.

[Page 179/180]

Episodes

A. Ben-Hayim
Tel-Aviv, Israel

The Jewish residents of Stavisht were very proud of the Count's estate. Stavisht could not be considered a Jewish small town like all the others – it had a source of prestige – the Count's estate.

In truth, the Count himself was there very rarely. He was like a small magpie on the roof, as the saying goes. However, Stavisht was his official residence and he had there a whole staff of officials and clerks who were called by the people in town "the nobility."

They lived in the nicest quarters and beautifully built houses surrounded by orchards, trees and flowers. In contrast, the Jewish part of town consisted of little houses without a sign of green, except for a few houses belonging to the very rich Jews who possessed (or it was thought that they possessed) a few thousand rubles.

My father, peace upon him, born in Stavisht, would often tell stories about the Count's estate. I remember a few of them:

Once, the Count, who traveled in many countries, bought an Arabian horse and asked to have it sent to Stavisht. Did he then lack for horses? He just wanted to have an Arabian horse, so he could boast about it to the neighboring nobles. Can you imagine what a Count would do just to lord it over others? And so the day came when the Arabian horse arrived in Stavisht along with its handler, an Arab with burning large eyes wearing wide black trousers.

I should here like to add some marginal notes. When my father told this story, when I was about nine or ten years old, in my childish fantasy I would imagine that it was Ishmael the son of Hagar whom Abraham had sent out of his house. The young Ishmael grew up in the desert without a father's supervision. He did not go to heder and was not taught by tutors. So he grew up a wild man. He ran around the desert and chased wild horses there. That is why the Arabian horses were so wild and swift.

And now we return to our story:

The Jews of town told how this horse and his handler had a private cabin aboard ship (how they knew this I do not know) as well as private cars in the various trains and then finally, a special coach to Stavisht. A special stall was set up on the Count's estate and a place for the handler to live. They prepared a festive banquet for the precious guests. Nobles and their wives came from all over the area and they all admired the beautiful horse with its slender delicate hooves.

It took a long time for the horse to adjust to its environment and the climate. Finally, one day, the Count mounted the richly saddled horse and rode out with great pride. Unfortunately, on his return, as he came to the gate of the town, his horse fell down dead.

Here is another story my father told: Once the Countess fell ill and the greatest physicians came from Kiev and they discovered that she should be fed with the milt of fish.

There was a river in Stavisht with wonderful fish. The Count ordered that many fish be caught and their milt was removed. But among them there were many fish that had roe, so these fish, along with the fish whose milt had been removed, were given to the local Jews for the Sabbath. The Jews of Stavisht had enough fish to last until after the Melave Malkah [the last Sabbath meal].

[Page 183/184]

Returned from the Other World...

by Yisrael Rubin
White Plains, New York

I, Yisrael Robtshanski, was born in the Raskashne, or as this village was called, Ksenzivke. I had six brothers and one sister. She died in Stavisht at the time of the First World War.

This event, which happened to me, I shall remember for the rest of my life.

It happened when the Revolution broke out and the Russian Army disintegrated. All the soldiers fled taking along whatever weapons they had to their native villages. Every gentile who could read and write a little became an officer and organized a band of young gentiles. Their motto was: "Bey Zhidov, Spasey Rasya!" [Beat the Jews, Save Russia]. That is how the pogroms began. They would attack small towns, organize raids and rob everything that came to hand.

The Jews of all the small towns in Ukraine lived in fear during this entire period. Some small towns organized self-defense groups, but they were not much help.

A small town had to live from something, so people risked their lives in order to travel to the fairs, Sunday in Krivselevke, Monday in Pyatigory, Tuesday in Stavisht and Thursday in Zhashkov.

And now I come to what happened to me. On a Thursday, I, and some others, traveled to the fair in Zhashkov. There was a bandit in that area named Kazakov. Around two o'clock in the afternoon Kazakov showed up with a band of 25 hooligans and they began to rob and to beat the Jews. Whoever opposed them was shot. While the bandits were robbing and snatching goods from each other, and thus occupied, their commander Kazakov stood in the middle of town and harangued the gentiles who had come to the fair, that all Jews were Communists and as soon as they got rid of all the Jews they would be rid of the Communists. The gentiles cried, "Hurray!"

Kazakov had a son who was about fourteen years old. He rode on a pony. He was not interested in robbing. He took out his saber, chased the Jews and beat them until they fell dead.

It is impossible to describe the tumult and the fear. People were running and screaming and did not know which way to turn. The bandits rampaged for a few hours and then left with their loot. They left the dead and wounded lying in the street.

I also ran, I do not know in which direction. In Zhashkov the bathhouse was at the edge of town. Next door was a gentile's dwelling. I ran into his barn, into the horse's stall, and hid under a pile of straw. I lay there for a few hours. The gentile did not even know I was there, he had gone to the fair. Through the cracks I could see what was doing outside, and when I saw people walking around, I knew that the bandits had left. Then I came out of the stall and went to the center of town to the Stavisht departure area. I cannot begin to describe what I saw there. The dead bodies had been laid out in two rows on the ground. The wounded had been given first aid. I will never forget the screaming and crying. Everyone was up the whole night. They were afraid that the bandits might return to town.

The night passed quietly. No one left town Friday morning. And, I need not add, of course no one would think of traveling on the Sabbath. God helped. Sunday, we found out from gentiles passing through that all was well in Stavisht. But there was no waggoner to take us back to Stavisht. Suddenly I saw a gentile from my village, Raskashne. His name was Ivan. I used to hire him to take eggs and flour to Belaya Tserkov and Kiev. It felt as if I had seen the Messiah! Even if he were not willing to drive me home, at least he could report back that I was still alive. I talked to him and he told me that his wagon was full of straw and that I should lie down under the straw and he would take me to Stavisht.

At home they had heard from some gentiles returning from the Zhashkov fair what had been going on there. Sunday morning my mother and brother Moshe began to look for a way to find out what had happened to me. We had a gentile neighbor named Petro. He was blind in one eye, lame in one foot, and was a drunkard as well. My brother Moshe hired Petro to drive to Zhashkov and find out what had happened to me. He was well paid and he left. Some readers may remember that the road between Stavisht and Zhashkov passed though a small wooded area. The trip took half a day. Petro came back and told my mother the "good news," that he had seen me and two other Jews hanging from trees in the woods.

He even described what I was wearing. There could be no doubt because he knew me, I had grown up in the house next door.

You can imagine the mourning and wailing in my home.

The Stavisht marketplace was on the highway opposite the Bet Hamidrash. That is where people bought and sold, discussed politics, hired laborers, or rented a carriage for transportation.

My mother and my brother ran to the highway. They were convinced that I was hanging in the woods, because who knew me better than Petro? My mother cried and screamed and a crowd gathered. I was well known in town because I conducted business with many people and often traveled to Kiev to sell eggs and flour and to bring back all kinds of products: textiles, sugar, salt, soap. Everything imported from Kiev has added value and it was profitable. Therefore everyone knew me quite well. In a small town everyone knows everyone else.

My mother did not stop crying. My brother Moshe and a few householders were ready to drive to the woods and take down the three corpses and bring them for a Jewish burial. But they could not set out immediately. First of all, it was a dangerous trip and secondly, they had to know the exact spot where the men were hanging. They had to ask Petro to lead them to the right place. But meanwhile, Petro had gotten drunk and had passed out, lying under his wagon. It was no use, he did not respond to their pleas.

Just then a wagon pulled by two horses came down the highway, the wheels of the wagon creaking loudy over the cobblestones, and who should appear there rising from the wagon bed, but yours truly…

I did not know the reason for the tumult. What had happened? I saw only that the marketplace was full of people. You can imagine the reaction when they saw me. Everyone stood as if turned to stone. I cannot describe what went on that day in town. I shall not forget that Sunday as long as I live!

And that is how it went in all of the towns of the Ukraine. I turned twenty, fell in love with Paule Abatovke, Leyb Yaneshivker's daughter. We were married and left for the long voyage to America. How we managed that voyage is a story in itself.

We came to the golden land and settled in a small town, White Plains, twenty miles from New York. We have lived here this whole while and have raised a family, two daughters and a son, whom we have given a fine education. Our daughters graduated from college and our son became a doctor and we are all happy together.

[Page 189/190]

Memories

by Hava Zaslavski
(daughter of Rabbi Yitshak-Avraham)

Stavisht was a small town in Ukraine, Province of Kiev where I was born, spent my childhood years and the best years of a person's life. The town of Stavisht was similar to hundreds of Ukrainian towns in all aspects: economic, intellectual, commercial. However, it was much prettier in its landscape. It was surrounded by great pine forests, beautiful flowing rivers, trees and fields. Its climate was healthy. Often Jews would come from larger cities to spend the summer in its healthful atmosphere.

There were 800-1000 Jewish families. The gentiles lived outside of town. Thus the Jews and the gentiles did not come into contact very much except for the one day a week when the latter would come with their produce to do business.

The Jews were mostly shopkeepers or artisans, brokers and idlers. There were very few rich people in Stavisht. Mostly they were middle class and the artisans were very poor. In general it was a poor town.

Nevertheless, the Jews were divided into various groups who had little to do with each other. Family prestige was of great importance. The children of the various strata went to different schools. The artisans were quite separate from the others, even lived in a different part of town, had their own synagogue, prayed with their own quorums. The children of the better classes were forbidden to play with artisans' children and, of course, there were no marriages between the classes.

Another group which was treated as outcasts was the Zionist group. They were of the younger generation, more worldly, more idealistic, and worked for Erets Yisrael. They had their own synagogue and kept apart from the pious Jews, who fought them bitterly. The pious Jews waited for God to lead them to Erets Yisrael.

There were six synagogues in town and many Jews sat and studied Torah day and night. They did not worry about making a living. The women provided. The women worked in the stores, traveled to the fairs in other towns, and the men prepared "the world to come."

However, there were no great scholars of renown in Stavisht. One of the few scholars was the Stavishter Rabbi, Rabbi Yitshak Avraham. Besides being a pious scholar, he was also very wise. He was the religious leader of the town, the adviser, the peacemaker, the representative of all the Jews before God and before the world. He helped the Jews of Stavisht at all times, especially in time of war. At the time of the pogroms he rescued them from the murderers' hands. With his great wisdom he saved the Jews from the greatest dangers. I remember that once the bandits gathered all the Jews in the Bet Hamidrash and were ready to set it on fire. The rabbi came out and started a discussion with the bandits and told the Jews to sneak out of the back door. When the bandits caught on to the ruse, there was no one left. They wanted to hang the rabbi. The gallows were ready and the rabbi was already standing on a bench when their leader came and took the rabbi home. He often risked his life to save the Jews of Stavisht and of other towns as well.

The town of Stavisht was isolated. It was located 50 viorst [about 33 miles] from the nearest train station. Jews who were knowledgeable and worldly wanted to know what was going on in the world. Every week the newspapers Hatsefira and Hazeman would arrive. The Jews were very politically aware and after the prayers they would spend hours in the synagogues discussing politics and figuring out who was going to go to war with whom, and who would win, when there would be a revolution and where kings would be deposed, and everything else going on in the world. The two newspapers were handed around and read all week long.

Stavisht was known as the place where Count Branicki had his estate. His nobles lived in Stavisht and provided an income for Jews and his estate beautified the town. The nobles lived around the Count's palace in beautiful modern houses surrounded by tall trees. In the middle was a boulevard where the Jews young and old promenaded on Sabbath and holidays.

Boys and girls would meet there, enjoy each other's company, and I am certain that all Stavishters remember that boulevard when they recall their youth.

There were no secular schools in Stavisht. All the children attended hadarim and received a religious education. The wealthier Jews would bring in private tutors from larger towns to teach their children secular subjects. The middle class enjoyed these benefits as well. After they had completed their studies, the young people would go to the large cities to take the examinations.

It is to our town's credit that all the youth strove for learning and Torah. The young people were also divided into classes. Almost all of the idealists were Zionists, who wanted to go to Erets Yisrael to build the land for the Jewish people. There were also socialists who dreamed of a revolution, deposing the Czar, and the rule of goodness in the world.

The young people dreamed of leaving the small town of Stavisht to study in the big cities, but very few succeeded in doing so.

Outstanding Personalities

[Page 201/202]

Outstanding Personalities

by Yisrael Rubin

Arthur Schechter

Arthur Schechter left Stavisht in 1907 when he was 14 years old. When he came to America he settled in Chicago where he lived for some years. In 1918 he came to Grand Rapids, Michigan where he has been living until the present.

Schechter started out buying hides, treating them, then selling them to big firms. The company's name is Wolverine Hide Company. He has built up his business to such an extent that not only does he sell his merchandise in the United States, but he also exports it abroad.

Even though he is very much involved in his business, Schechter finds time for community work and is active in all aspects of Jewish life, especially in the field of Jewish culture. He is a member of various Jewish organizations, for example, the Jewish Culture Congress, YIVO, vice-president of the Jewish Labor Committee, representative in his city of the United Jewish Appeal, and chairman of the Israel Bond Campaign in his city and vicinity.

I know him personally. I remember him from the Old Country and am very close to him here. He is also a member of the Workmen's Circle of the United States and Canada of which I am also a member. We often see each other at meetings of the various organizations to which we both belong. Moreover, he is a great philanthropist with a good soul and a kind heart. He helps everyone, and whenever help is needed, with a generous hand.

I feel that it would be a great injustice if I did not write to express what I know and feel about my friend Arthur Schechter. Here is an example of his generosity. When he was in New York a few years ago, he proposed to me and some other Stavisht landslayt that we memorialize our town by writing a book about the Stavisht of our times. We were immediately inspired by this idea and called a meeting of our landslayt and chose a committee to carry out this project. Schechter was not only the initiator of the idea, but he was its greatest financial supporter. Without his initiative and support we would not have been able to carry out this wonderful memorial project of our town Stavisht.

Schechter is a dear man with great love for Jews, Jewish culture, Jewish literature, and even more, for Stavisht and Stavisht landslayt. He works for Jewish causes with enthusiasm. He is a real Ukrainian Stavisht Hasid. We are proud of him and we wish him and his family long years of fruitful communal work.

Moshe Galant

Among those who should be mentioned for their active role in pushing forward the project of writing this book is Moshe Galant, Moshe Katsebivker's step-son.

I should also mention some other Stavisht landslayt who helped him become the person he is. One of those is the teacher, Isaac Lande, who came to Stavisht and became a teacher in the Talmud Torah. Moshe Galant was one of his students. Lande saw great promise in him. He involved himself in Moshe's education. However, Lande did not remain in his position as teacher for long. He was hired by the estate of Count Branicki to serve as a secretary in the office there.

Lande suggested to Moshe that he come to his home, where he and his sister, Sonia, tutored him privately. Moshe learned much from Lande, as well as from his step-father, Moshe Katsebivker. Later he became an assistant to Moshe the melamed and helped to teach the children their blessings, reviewed the morning prayers with them as well as other subjects taught in the lower grades.

Leyzer Motelivker suggested to Moshe that he come to the village of Motelivke to tutor Leyzer's children. Moshe spent one semester there earning nine rubles for his labors. He returned to Stavisht and became a frequent visitor at the Lande home, drinking in as much knowledge as he could. He understood that there was no future there for him. With only 13 rubles in this pocket he left Stavisht and came to Skvira to study.

Galant had a grandfather in Skvira, a very pious Jew, an important man in the community who served as cantor in the big synagogue. When he found out that his grandson was attending a government school, he drove him out of his house. Moshe's 13 rubles were spent and he was destitute.

The pupils in the government school where Galant was enrolled found out about his situation and told their parents. The parents, together with the government appointed rabbi and his brother-in-law, the town doctor, decided to help Moshe by providing him with meals, every family taking him for a week in turn. Galant found himself in a fine, aristocratic environment. After he completed his studies he went to Kiev.

In Kiev he found a position in a lawyer's office. He returned to Stavisht and became a second Lande. Lande saw that the education he had provided for Moshe had not been in vain.

Galant became a teacher of Russian in the school of Shemuel the melamed. After a time he opened his own private school where both Jewish and Christian children attended. Among the non-Jewish children in attendance were the children of the feldsher [paramedic] Khartshinski, the lawyer Satshinski, and even the children of the police commissioner.

The Skvira police commander was transferred to the Tarashcha Uyezd. He met Galant at the home of the police commissioner and recognized him. He used to see him at the homes of aristocratic families in Skvira where Galant was nicknamed "Dos Yingele" [The young boy]. He suggested to Galant that he give up teaching and referred him to the owner of the sugar factory in Zhashkov. Galant got a job in the factory office. The factory functioned only three months every year, but Galant kept the job for six months. He became acquainted with a well-known lawyer, Tshudnovski, a sickly man who needed someone like Galant who was skilled in law, and he took him on as an assistant.

Tshudnovski died and Galant took over his office and his clients. The owner of the sugar factory was also a lawyer, but did not have time for his law business so he hired Galant to take care of it.

When the unrests and pogroms started in Ukraine, Galant moved to Bessarabia (then part of Romania). He became acquainted with editors of periodicals in Romanian, Yiddish, and Russian, and became involved in administrative work at these periodicals. He earned a fine income, bought a house, raised a family, and lived there until news came that Hitler would occupy Bessarabia.

His daughter in America sent him the necessary papers and he left Bessarabia and came to America. In New York he was warmly welcomed by the Stavisht landslayt. He settled in America and became a successful businessman.

At out last meeting, on March 19, Galant participated in the Maot Hitin campaign [funds to help the needy during Passover]. Although he is 78 years old, he is the same lively and vibrant Moshe Galant as he was in this youth.

Yisrael Senderovitsh

Yisrael Senderovitsh of Toronto, Canada, came here as a young boy and settled in Canada. He married, raised a family, and was always devoted to the interests of our landslayt and to our old home town of Stavisht.

With the help of some landslayt he founded a landsmanshaft [a Jewish benefit or hometown group] society and was the president of the society for many years, until his wife became ill and he could no longer devote himself to its affairs.

Little by little the older members departed and the younger ones were not interested or connected to the old country. Neighborhoods changed and many people moved to new homes and the society disbanded. Nevertheless, Yisrael Senderovitsh remained faithfully devoted with heart and soul to his landslayt and he would meet and spend time with them on various occasions.

When the idea of creating a memorial book about Stavisht came from New York to Canada, he was the first to take part in the work and he immediately responded that he was ready to help in any way he could. He himself did not write any articles because he was very young when he came to Canada and did not remember much about Stavisht.

He recently lost his wife and did not have the inclination to write, but he helped in any way he could to further the work. He met with some of the landslayt and they decided to raise a sum of money to help fund the publication of the book.

He sent the contribution to our committee with a letter expressing his feelings of sympathy for the sacred task. Therefore the committee wishes to express its heartfelt gratitude to our friend Yisrael Senderovitsh and to the other members of the committee who volunteered their efforts to create a book as a memorial for our home town of Stavisht.

Shelomo (Solomon) Golub

Shelomo Golub Beraze was a Yiddish teacher in Russia. He was a very educated man belonging to the Zionist organization. When he was young he gave private lessons to the children of householders in Stavisht.

We were a group of four boys: Levi Pritsker, the son of Mordekhai the chandler [candle maker and seller]; Eliyahu Rozenblit, the son of Nahman the Palnamats [holder of special privileges]; Yotek Kohen, the son of Eliyahu Yaakov-Yisrael the butcher; and I myself, Yisrael Rubtshinski, the son of Yehoshua'ke the butcher. We were between 12 and 15 years old. We had left the hadorim where we had studied for many years, beginning with elementary studies and ending with Pentateuch with Rashi commentary and Talmud.

We suggested to Solomon Golub that he teach us four boys two to three hours a day. We studied with him for two years. He was logical, organized, and tactful and he knew how to approach us and how to gain the trust of his students.

Sometime later he gave up the teaching profession and became a businessman. He rented a store where he sold books and office supplies. He did good business up until the time we left Stavisht.

The Golub family raised fine, well-educated sons with good characters and good hearts. After the First World War and the Revolution, when the upheavals began and the various forces and bands of bandits came in, it was impossible to remain in Stavisht. They decided to leave and come to America. The journey was not so simple. They spent some time in Odessa, then a longer time in Bessarabia, Romania, until the miracle occurred and they came to America.

Shelomo (Solomon) Golub

[*Translator's note:* He was my mother's teacher
and we visited him once, in the Bronx or Upper Manhattan,
when I was a little girl.]

This happened to all the emigrants who suffered a great deal before they found their place of rest. In the golden land of America they also struggled for a while, but in a relatively short time they had established themselves.

The oldest son is an insurance agent and involves himself in communal work, and supported his father and mother for a long time in the finest way. One can say that he fulfilled the commandment, "Honor your father and mother" to the utmost. The second son has a fruit business and has a fine family. The third son, the kindhearted Sonny, works for the New York Times and also has a fine family.

Returning to Shelomo Golub, I want to say that the past few years were difficult for him. He had lost his vision and could not continue his communal work as he wished. He reached a ripe old age. He died in 1960 at age 87, his wife having died a few years earlier.

This a brief biography of a noble, fine landsman of the town Stavisht.

Moshe-Leyb (Morris) Kanski

He was still quite young at the time of the First World War. Then came the Revolution and after that as the regimes changed hands, band after band of pogromchiks would come and terrorize Stavisht. Moshe-Leyb felt a strong need to defend his town in any way he could.

At that time a self-defense force of young people, with our Rabbi Yitshak Avraham Gasinski at its head, was founded. They would go around at night to protect the town. Moshe-Leyb participated in the night watch and thanks to him the town was often saved from attack.

As a young man Moshe-Leyb wanted to leave Russia and go to America as many other Jews had done. He became acquainted with a girl who lived across the street, Gitl Zshivatovski, daughter of Godel-Hersh Hanna. In a short time they were married and left for America.

They settled in New York and he began to sell textiles, the same kind of business he had in Stavisht. He started on a small scale but eventually opened a store where he was very successful. He was observant, prayed every day, kept a Jewish home, but he was not a fanatic. He was an honorable person in every sense of the word. He never cheated anyone, never took money from anybody. He observed the axiom: What is mine is mine and what is yours is yours.

He joined the Stavisht landsmanshaft and became very active, devoted heart and soul to the membership and the society. He was a trustee and a candidate for president. He was friendly with all the landslayt and was loved and respected by all. He had a good character, liked to do favors for people, people used to come to ask his advice, and he would advise them to the best of his ability.

Moshe-Leyb (Morris) Kanski

But no one knows what tomorrow will bring. Even though he was only middle aged, he began to feel ill. He began to withdraw from business and from other activities and about three months ago he drew his last breath, at the age of 61. It was a great loss for the Stavisht landslayt and they will never forget him. Honor to his memory!

Documents

[Page 221/222]

Pogrom Happenings in Stavisht

by Yisrael Rubin

Stavisht is a town in the Uyezd of Tarashcha, near the River Ikaash [note: in Russian the name of the river is Gniloii Tikich, a branch of the Bug River.], fifty viorst [about 33 miles] from a train station (Belaya Tserkov station). In 1917 it had about 20,000 Christian inhabitants and 6,000 Jews. At present there are about 80 Jewish families, about 400 people. It had one brandy distillery, three mills, a seltzer water factory, various artisans, and commercial enterprises.

Before the Revolution the relations between Christians and Jews were neutral, neither friendly nor hostile. In 1905, when there was an outbreak of pogroms in the area, it was quiet in Stavisht. Before the Revolution the following organizations existed: a savings and loan society, a credit union, six cooperative stores, a Talmud Torah, a Jewish school with two grades and a government school with four grades.

In October 1917, on one of the market days, a pogrom broke out led by demobilized soldiers. The textile shop of H. Ulanovski was robbed. The pogrom lasted several hours. It was quelled thanks to the local militia which played an important role in defending the town.

In November of that same year a band of 18 men entered the town, led by a man named Dabravalski. These were bandits whose only goal was robbery. They demanded and received a "contribution" of 15,000 rubles and left after two hours.

In February of 1918, at the time of the Central Council, a band of 200 men burst into the town and took control. At its head was Kravtshenko, from the village of Snizshke. The Ukrainian militia arrived to drive them out and they robbed several stores.

In 1918, a few thousand peasants from the village of Strizivke began a pogrom against Jews whom they accused of bringing in the Germans. On the way to Stavisht they killed about 25 Jews; in the village of Strizivke they killed 14 Jews; in the village of Sukhari 67 Jews; and another five on the way. More peasants joined from the village of Tartsitse. At their head was a well-known Bolshevik, Gribenko. They took over the power in Stavisht and neighboring villages. They stayed there until August. On August 17 there was a battle between the peasants and the Germans, who drove Gribenko out of town. The peasants killed six Jews in their retreat from Stavisht. Of those killed we know the names of Avraham-Eli Levin and Yitshak Tori.

From that time the town was cut off from commercial enterprise. No Jew could leave town for the woods and roads were full of partisans who robbed and killed Jews passing through. This was the situation in 1919.

During the intermediate days of Passover 1919 a band of 80 soldiers came into town. They called themselves "Bazinevtes." They robbed for a few hours, but their leaders forced them to return to the Jewish population that which they had taken and they gave back a great deal. On the second day of Shavuot in 1919 a band of 5,000 men came into town. This was a unit from Griogrive's militia. The leaders were Yatsenko and Zsheliezniak. They stayed in town eleven days. On the first day there were six Jews killed, of whom we know the names of the following: David Kohen, 20 years old; Yitshak Kohen, 30 years old; Ben Tsiyon Maldavanski, 43 years old; Svirski [or Szirski] 18 years old. They demanded one million rubles or they would slaughter the entire Jewish population. Only 500,000 rubles could be collected. They also took 30 head of cattle, 30 horses and wagons. Throughout the eleven days they were in town they robbed the Jews taking whatever merchandise they could find. They murdered the head of the Committee of the Poor, Mordekhai Gutharts, killed two visiting Jews, and raped many women. They arrested ten Jews on trumped up charges that the Jews had shot at them. Thanks to Rabbi Avraham, the rabbi of Stavisht, who risked his life to go to them and mollified them, the prisoners were freed. Zsheliezniak said that they were only against Communists. On the twelfth day they left for Tarashcha where they were badly beaten by the Red Army and they retreated back to Stavisht. This happened on June 15, 1919. They stayed in town from early morning until two in the afternoon and killed 30 Jews.

They left at two o'clock. A few days later they started to come back to town, but the Jews had learned of their approach and they fled. Most of them fled to Volodarke, Skvira Uyezd, about 18 viorst away. Many fled to Belaya Tserkov and others to nearby villages. The bandits robbed the abandoned Jewish homes in Stavisht and then made their way to Voladarke where they found the greatest number of Stavisht Jews. Rabbi Avraham went to the leader, Zsheliezniak, who had great respect for him. All of the Stavisht Jews were allowed to return home. On their way to Voladarke, the bandits had burned the bridge over the Rasi River. They forced the local peasants to bring boards to serve as a temporary bridge over which the Stavisht Jews crossed on their way home. Zsheliezniak even gave the Jews bread for the journey.

One night in July 1919, the military commissar Karnivski and his assistant Baytshkovski, both born in the village of Flark (10 viorst from Stavisht), and his Red Army unit of 20 men broke into several Jewish homes, broke the windows, broke down the doors, and robbed and killed nine people. Of the dead the following are known: Sara Royzenblit, 45 years old with two daughters, 18 and 20 years old; Ze'ev Vaynshthein, 40 years old; Beyla Vekslin, a dentist, 50 years old; Ya'akov Ber Zshivotovski. They wanted to burn down all the Jewish homes and they notified the peasants of the neighboring villages that they should come and help them get rid of the Jews. Two wagonloads of peasants came, but ten local peasants opposed them and defended the town. Two days later Commissar Mazali came from Tarashcha to put down the uprising and they too robbed many Jewish homes. Karnivski and his unit came a number of times. One Sabbath he announced that if the Jews did not come to defend themselves against the charge that they had complained about him in Kiev, he would cut off the town. He called the Rabbi, who did not come. The local militia took strenuous measures to defend the town.

On the fourth of Av 1919, a band of 12,000 followers of Zelenovtse came into town. They demanded two million rubles and merchandise. They received 412,000 rubles and 20 head of cattle. They robbed and took whatever was left, whatever had been hidden. They killed two people. One of them was Mordekhai Frenkel. Before they received the contribution they arrested 30 people, among whom were: Rabbi Avraham, Binyamin Faynzilber, Khlavna Kohen, Shemuel Salganik, Yosef Stepanski, and yours truly. One of the officers took a great deal of money from the Jews in addition to the contribution and did not allow more to be killed.

Rosh Hashanah eve 1919 Dobrovolski and 20 men came into town and demanded 100,000 rubles threatening that he would kill and rob if he did not get the money. They received 65,000 rubles and did not hurt anyone. However, when the Jewish representatives came to ask that his band not rob anyone he shot at them, but did not hit them.

In November 1919 a group of 16 followers of Denikin came into town. They demanded a "contribution." They were given 70,000 rubles. They took a lot of gold and silver and killed and robbed. They raped two women in the Bet Hamidrash and killed a 70 year old woman, Kapatshevski, who was bringing her share of the contribution. In the Bet Hamidrash they took everyone's clothing, examined them, and took everything away, leaving the people naked. They beat them unmercifully. They wanted to chop off Rabbi Avraham's right hand, but he begged and pleaded so much that they did not. Then they were going to hang him on the hook of the hanging lamp but decided not to. They demanded that food and liquor be brought to the Bet Hamidrash and as they ate and drank they called out, "Long life to the Christians and death to the Jews!"

In December 1919, when the Denikins left Ukraine, many militia units came through Stavisht and robbed and pillaged. On the tenth of December a group of 20 men came through and demanded 20,000 rubles. On the 12th of December 1919, 40 peasants came with Denikin's militia. They came to the Bet Hamidrash with a note from the commandant, took 50,000 rubles contribution, ten pud [about 360 lbs.] of oats and other goods. On the 15th of December a large group of Denikin's militia came through and robbed the Jews. There were three killed of whom we know the names of two: Reuven Fishlin and Mirashnik. A four year old child, Nathan, was seriously wounded, as well as an old man, Reuven Banin. They hung him up three times, yet he remained alive. They raped many women and set fire to many houses. Three houses belonging to Shalom Tripolski, Moshe Kohen, and Yosef Binyamin Broytman were burned to the ground.

Until April 1920 all was quiet, but even in the relatively quiet times between pogroms the local militia would carry out attacks on Jewish houses and rob them. Then, on the 20th of April 1920, a band of 50 men led by Slipanski and Karavski, natives of the village of Handikha, came from Tetiev. The Jews had learned of their approach and had fled a day earlier. They ran towards Tarashcha, Vinograd and Belaya Tserkov. A few old, sick and disabled people remained behind. The bandits killed 18 people of whom the following are known: Sara Shapira, Avraham Aba Tshubinski. They wanted to set fire to the town but some of the local Christians did not allow this. They stayed for two days and left. Eight days later some of them came back and robbed and pillaged. There was a man from Stavisht in their group, who had served in the Stavisht militia, and he did not allow them to kill anyone. This time they stayed for three days. A few days later some of them came back and demanded that all the Jews leave within two hours. They brought all the Jewish residents to the Polish commandant and took them seven viorst from town to the village of Krivets and then told them to go wherever they wished. Only the sick and disabled remained in town.

Then the local peasants took advantage of the situation and stole everything possible. There was a Polish authority in town which did nothing to stop them. One eye-witness, Monus Marianovski, had a Polish passport, and the authority told him to leave town saying that they would not be responsible for his life. At that time the bandits killed 18 people, among whom were: Sara Kaplavtsker, Shalom Landsman, and Shelomo Zalman Frenkel. In the Jewish Bikur Holim [hospital] they killed six old women. They killed Frenkel by tying him to a pig, throwing the pig into a cellar and then setting the cellar on fire, burning him and the pig alive.

About eight days after Shavuot, when the Poles left, the local peasants entered many houses and robbed them. It became a bit quieter and a few people returned. Some of the local Christian intelligentsia took part in the robberies. Among them were: Tsherbin, a teacher in the Stavisht four grade school; the justice of the peace, who started a panic every day saying the bandits were coming so that people would run away. The inspector of the four grade school invented a false charge that the Jewish Communists were coming to Stavisht to kill the Christians. They encircled the town with machine guns and the local Christians joined the bandits and pillaged. On one day in June they set five houses on fire.

There are now about 80 Jewish families left in Stavisht. They are extremely fearful and are ready to flee at a moment's notice. The destruction is great. All the stores are closed, there is absolutely no business going on. Most homes are wrecked.

Sh. Rabinovits wrote this for Khlavna Kagan, former member of the Stavisht Town Authority, who could not write because it was Rosh Hashanah.

Traianovski (?) [the question mark appears in the text]

[Page 235/236]

A Letter of Alarm

From the Rabbi of Stavisht to the Rabbi of Kiev
[Written in Hebrew]

Stavisht, 5 Elul, 5678 [August 13, 1918]

To his honor the honored and learned rabbi of the congregation of Kiev and environs Rabbi Shelomo Aharonson, the priest of God on high.

Peace!

We, the representatives of the Jews in Stavisht pour forth our pleas to you, our rabbi, to stand by us in this hour of mortal danger, which hovers over us, for of the ten measures of suffering which have been inflicted on the Jews of Ukraine in this time of emergency, nine measures have come upon us.

Our isolated town, fifty viorst from the railroad, is in the center of the land where the partisan uprising is happening. About six weeks ago our town was filled with the sound of army boots of the partisans, with Gribenko at their head. They declared a draft of all men aged eighteen to forty. Afterwards they lay a fine upon our town of 15,000 rubles. They were given all of the money and they nullified the draft order. They confiscated much merchandise for which they sometimes paid a small sum. There is almost no shop in town which has not suffered from this confiscation.

In the early period the partisans seemed to be satisfied with taking money and merchandise and did not cause violence and the spilling of blood, because there was a certain amount of discipline imposed by their leaders to whom we could turn for protection. However now the situation has completely changed. Two weeks ago a group of Germans came to town and the partisans left. On the second day a battle began between the two camps. It started outside of Stavisht but little by little the partisans were forced to retreat into the town and the narrow streets became killing fields. For seven hours without cease there was thunder of rifles and grenades and a rain of fire on the town. Of the Jews there were four dead and many wounded because the bullets of death penetrated the walls into the houses. But our most terrible sufferings began after the battle.

The leaders and some of the partisans retreated and left our area and found refuge on the other side of the Dnieper. However, a large portion of them, peasants from the area, returned to their homes, hid their arms, and posed as peasants going about their work. The Germans could not find them because their families would not give them up. The Germans stayed in town for five days and as soon as they left the partisans removed their disguises, took up their arms, and became the rulers. Since they had no leaders, they were simply a band of robbers and murderers. They would gather into bands of ten or more men, lay ambushes on the roads and kill all the Jews passing by after taking everything they had. Every day one or two dead Jews are brought into town. No one dares to leave for fear of these bandits.

The sources of income have been stopped and the lives of the residents hang by a thread. The bands are not satisfied with ambush only, but invade the town, band by band, armed with swords, rifles, and grenades; they attack the houses and rob them, enter the stores and take merchandise, then require tribute from the town.

For example, On Sunday, this week, a band of eleven bandits came into town, armed with grenades, and demanded a tribute of 25,000 rubles. After much begging by the rabbi, in tears, they lowered the sum to 15,000 rubles. They gave us one hour to collect the money. Now there is a rumor that they are planning to set fire to the whole town, after they have plundered it. Our small community is in the midst of tens of villages filled with murderers and robbers, armed to the teeth. We are like a lamb ringed by seventy wolves. We are poor and without weapons to defend ourselves. Have mercy, Rabbi, on our unfortunate community, and send us assistance in our time of trouble. Let the authorities know that they must send us a defense force immediately, for death awaits us and our wives and children, horrible death by sword and fire.

We have been informed that a German unit is approaching but will be here only a few days, and afterwards the bandits will again wreak havoc upon us. We ask and plead in the name of one thousand Jewish families for help. Please send us a permanent defense force so that the Germans will not just come in and out for they do nothing to prevent the violence and the robbery.

So says the member of the juridical authority (signature)

So says Yitshak Avraham Haysinski, Rabbi of Stavisht (signature)

P.S. Since the letter has been delayed until today, the tenth of Elul, more dead bodies have been gathered that were found on the roads. Yesterday they found nine dead Jews, five men and four women, near the village Zshidivsko Grebli. In another place there were dead gentiles. Even though the Germans are in town and protect it against attack, the roads are still dangerous.

(Received August 23, 1918)

[Page 239/240]

Forward, December 30, 1920, no. 8473:

Names of One Hundred Murdered Jews in Stavisht, Province of Kiev

[Note: I have transliterated the names as they appear in text]

Special cable to the Forward from N. Shifrin, Berlin, December 29. "I have received the names of over one hundred murdered Jews in Stavisht, Kiev Province."

The following have left behind a wife and four children:

1. Avraham'l Litvak, 40 years old.
2. Ben-Tsiyon Maladavski, 46 years old.
3. His son, Reuven.
4. Meir the teacher, 38 years old.
5. Mikhl Papirovitsh, 55 years old.
6. Ya'akov the ritual slaughterer, 40 years old.
7. Nahum the carpenter, 55 years old.

The following have left behind a wife and five children:

8. Binyamin Natavski, from Yanashivke, 35 years old.
9. Shmulik Stavski, 45 years old.
10. His wife, 38 years old.
11. Mordekhai Leyb Frenkel, 45 years old.
12. Avraham the ritual slaughterer, 55 years old.
13. His wife, 50 years old.

The following have left behind a wife and six children:

14. Tsevi Grabman, 44 years old.
15. Shalom Shvetkay, 28 years old.

The following have left behind a wife and one or two children:

16. Tsevi Lazanski, 40 years old.
17. Avraham Dvinski, 35 years old.
18. Gitl Senderovski, 35 years old.
19. Esther, Kalman the hatter's daughter, 60 years old.
20. Mordshe Berkum, 48 years old.
21. Bayets Berkum, 22 years old.
22. Meir, 16 years old.
23. Ele Stepanski, 35 years old.
24. His brother Mendl 23 years old.
25. Yitshak Kagan, 35 years old.
26. Motl Fishman, 28 years old.
27. Avraham Meir Fishman, 38 years old.
28. Nahum Frants, 33 years old.
29. Fayvish Platinski, 55 years old.
30. Tittsek the miller, 55 years old.
31. Khvelye Dartshevski, 40 years old.
32. Motl Gutharts, 35 years old.
33. Volke (Zeev) Vaynshteyn, 45 years old.
34. Fayvl the blacksmith, 45 years old.
35. His son, David, 28 years old.
36. Veksler the dentist, 40 years old.
37. His wife, Belah.
38. Hershl the cobbler, 35 years old.
39. Ayzik Kanski, 58 years old.
40. Shalom Denest, 55 years old.
41. Avraham'l the shingler, 50 years old.
42. Asher the water-carrier's step-son, 30 years old.
43. His wife.
44. David Itsik's, 32 years old.
45. Shalom Salganik, 55 years old.
46. Jacob Grinshpan, 35 years old.
47. Stapla, wife of Ben-Tsiyon the teacher, 35 years old.
48. Hayke, 15 years old.

49. Zelde, 5 years old.
50. Rahel, 9 years old, wounded,
51. Feyge, 4 years old.
52. Baby, 2 years old.
53. Nahum Velvel Berdshadski, 60 years old.
54. His brother Yonah, 50 years old.
55. Meir Miratshnik, 55 years old.
56. Hanah Meszibovskaya, 50 years old.
57. Yaakov David Zshivatavski, 60 years old.
58. Levi the waggoner, 30 years old.
59. Moshe Shelomoh Kushnier, 25 years old.
60. Unknown young man.
61. Mahlah Kaptshevskaya, 70 years old.
62. Avraham, son of David the [platatshnik], 12 years old.
63. Ayzik Rizanski, 55 years old.
64. Avraham Sukanik, 75 years old.
65. Yankl Shumski's mother, 70 years old.
66. Gitl Rive Krasilavskaya, 75 years old.
67. Yosl Zshabtshinkski, 75 years old.
68. His wife, 70 years old.
69. Zeydl Volodarski, 25 years old.
70. Avraham Aba (Efrayim Tshudinski's son?), 30 years old.
71. Beni, son of Aharon the tailor, 22 years old.
72. Pine, son of Yeruham, 8 years old.
73. An old lame woman, "Di Litvatshke," 75 years old.
74. Daughter of Avraham the ritual slaughterer, 20 years old.
75. Itsik Tori, 40 years old.
76. David, son of the shingler, 25 years old.
77. Tsevi Pisnay, from Stanislantshik, 16 years old.
78. Gessl son of Yisrael Yonah, 22 years old.
79. Yankl Grafman, 25 years old.
80. Avraham Shestak, 23 years old.
81. Tsevi Zagatavshtshik, from Rakitina, 45 years old.
82. Yitshak Shatshan, 23 years old.
83. Pesye Kartshevskaia, 55 years old.
84. Sarah Rozenberg (Rosenblit?), 45 years old.
85. Her daughter Hanah, 22 years old.
86. Her daughter, 18 years old.
87. Shime Boyarski, 35 years old.
88. Shelomoh Zalman the galoshes maker, 75 years old.
89. Moshe Nesyer the coppersmith, 20 years old.
90. Sarah Shapira, 55 years old.
91. Ittse Mazeraki, 50 years old.
92. Golde Dikstevitsh, 50 years old.
93. Mother (Sara?) of Pittse Kaplavitsh, 70 years old.
94. Lipe Stepanski, 60 years old.
95. Avraham son of Moshe Yankl, 20 years old.
96. Kalman Nahum the carpenter, 25 years old.
97. His bride, 20 years old.
98. Berl Yaladarski, blind, 80 years old.

99. Sarah the brunette, a disabled woman, 80 years old.
100. Sarah the waitress, 80 years old.
101. Alte the weaver's daughter, 30 years old.
102. Her husband, 32 years old.

Another two dead that I know about:

1. Yosef Rubtshinski the butcher, 87 years old.
2. His wife, Batya, 84 years old.

[*Translator's note*: The references below seem to be inconsistent with the dates and descriptions in other previous essays.]

These are the last martyrs who were murdered by Zshelezniak's band in the big Bet Hamidrash, possibly the last Jews in town.

1.	Levin, Avraham-Eli	Murdered in August 1918.
2.	Kohen, David, 20	Murdered in 1919.
3.	Szirski, 18.	Murdered in 1919.
4.	Fishlin, Reuven	Murdered in 1920.
5.	Landsman, Shalom	Murdered in 1920.
6.	Fren[k]el, Shelomo Zalman	Murdered in 1920.
7/8.	Smalier and his wife	(Burned alive in their home)

All of these documents were Photostats given to us by YIVO (Eliahu Tsherikover collection).

The committee wishes to express its heartfelt gratitude to YIVO of New York for collecting the historic data about our town and giving us the Photostats.

[Page 245/246]

סֵפֶר
מִשְׁפַּט הַקּוֹרֵא
כולל כל דרכי הנקוד ומשפטי הקריאה בתורה לכל פרשיהם והקדוזיהם
מאת לוי בן אליעזר מנחם ספעקטער .
ס"ץ וקורא בעיר סטאוישט פלך קיאב
הולבהלד ע"י דוד הורוויץ באדסא

אדעססא
בדפוס א. רובן
שנת תרנ"ו לפ"ק

י"ל מחדש ע"י
בן בתר של המחבר ז"ל
דוד קאהן

The Book <u>Mishpat Hakore</u>

**Reb Levi son of Eliezer Menahem Spekter
author of <u>Mishpat Hakore</u>.**

[*Translator's note:* This photo is juxtaposed with the
title page of book <u>Mishpat Hakore</u> (Odessa: David
Horovitz, 1896).
My mother spelled her father's name Spector.]

[Page 249/250]

Meeting of Book-Committee

January 12, 1961

The meeting was opened by Mr. Rubin. In attendance were Havah Zaslavski, Mr. Rubin, Mr. Palant, Mr. and Mrs. Louie Lipovski, Mr. and Mrs. Golub, Y. Golub.

Subjects under discussion:

1. To print the book in Israel;
2. To advertise in newspapers;
3. Photographs;
4. Fund raising;
5. Collection materials.

It was decided:

1. To use all of the materials and all of the photographs – as well as a photograph of the committee.
2. To print the book in Israel.
3. To advertise in Der Tog and Forverts.
4. To form a committee consisting of the following people: Galant, Rubin, Lipovski, and Y. Golub, who would meet with Stavisht landslayt and collect funds for the book.
5. Mr. Rubin presented a report on the materials which had come in – 19 articles, 26 pages from YIVO, and a list of names of 109 martyrs. Mr. Rubin also presented a list of articles which were due to be sent in.

[Signed by]

Moshe Galant
Hava Zaslavski
Louis Lipovski
Esther Lipovski
(Yitshak) Irving Golub
(Yosef) Joe Golub
Sonny Golub
Yisrael Rubin

Academy Hall, January 12, 1961.

[Page 251/252]

A Letter from Landslayt in Canada

We, the undersigned landslayt from Toronto and Montreal, Canada, greet the honorary president Arthur Schechter and the committee for the wonderful initiative to carry out a project of publishing a book about our town Stavisht. This is a noble and humanitarian undertaking and we were pleased to assist in this project in any way we could.

We have high regards for this task and we thank you very much for giving us the opportunity to participate in the work. We wish you great success in our cooperative effort.

[Signed]

Yisrael Senderovitsh
Y. Lavet
B. Yalavski
Y. Rayzman
M. Barinski
L. Smit
B. Hofman
B. Dubinski
S. Barsuk
M. Gulka
N. Yakubovitsh
Y. Miratshnik
Y. Pisnoy
B. Yakubovitsh
Dubah Sheynis-Smit

NAME INDEX